Energy and Agriculture in the Third World

WITHDRAWN FROM
THE LIBRARY

UNIVERSITY OF
WINCHESTER

KA 0009840 X

A Report to the Energy Policy Project of the Ford Foundation

Energy and Agriculture in the Third World

Arjun Makhijani
with the collaboration of **Alan Poole**

Ballinger Publishing Company ● Cambridge, Mass.
A Subsidiary of J.B. Lippincott Company

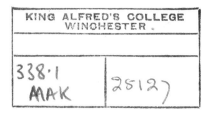

KING ALFRED'S COLLEGE
WINCHESTER .

338·1
MAK   28127

 This book is printed on recycled paper.

Published in the United States of America by Ballinger Publishing Company,
Cambridge, Mass.

First Printing, 1975

Copyright © 1975 by The Ford Foundation. All rights reserved. No part of
this publication may be reproduced, stored in a retrieval system, or transmitted
in any form or by means, electronic, mechanical, photocopy, recording or
otherwise, without the prior written consent of the publisher.

Library of Congress Catalog Card Number: 75-4777

International Standard Book Number: 0-88410-341-2 HB
0-88410-342-0 PB

Printed in the United States of America

Library of Congress Cataloging in Publication Data

Makhijani, Arjun.
   Energy and agriculture in the third world.

   Includes bibliographical references.
   1. Underdeveloped areas—Agriculture. 2. Underdeveloped areas—Income.
3. Underdeveloped areas—Economic policy. I. Poole, Alan, 1946-   joint
author. II. Title.
HD1417.M34 1975   338.1'09172'4   75-4777
ISBN 0-88410-341-2
ISBN 0-88410-342-0 pbk.

Contents

List of Figures

List of Tables

Foreword

In December 1971 the Trustees of the Ford Foundation authorized the organization of the Energy Policy Project. In subsequent decisions the Trustees have approved supporting appropriations to a total of $4 million, which is being spent over a three-year period for a series of studies and reports by responsible authorities in a wide range of fields. The Project Director is S. David Freeman, and the Project has had the continuing advice of a distinguished Advisory Board chaired by Gilbert White.

This analysis of "Energy and Agriculture in the Third World" is one of the results of the Project. As Mr. Freeman explains in his Preface, neither the Foundation nor the Project presumes to judge the specific conclusions and recommendations of the author who prepared this volume. We do commend this report to the public as a serious and responsible analysis which has been subjected to review by a number of qualified readers.

This study is rather different from others in the Project, in that it deals primarily with the problems and prospects of the developing countries. Its message is directed toward development planners and public administrators in the developing countries, and to virtually all donor agencies—including this Foundation—whose development assistance programs have yet to give adequate attention to the relationships between effective agricultural development and energy use. The new realities of the world energy situation make these relationships distressingly critical for the present and future, and all of us in this business must give immediate attention to their implications for development programs.

Because of the importance of this subject, and the uniqueness of the perspective of the author, I fully support the Project Director's decision to publish this study and give it full exposure as soon as possible. However, as many of our independent reviewers have reminded us, the relationship between energy and agriculture in developing countries is a large and complex subject, where data are scarce, technologies are in a state of rapid development, and social, political, and economic difficulties have a way of appearing where least expected. Neither the Foundation nor the author would claim that this study is more than a preliminary investigation of the subject, which will raise as many questions as it answers. If it is successful in stimulating active thought and good research on the questions it raises, it will have served the basic objective of the Energy Policy Project. In this spirit, I commend this analysis to the attention of those concerned with energy policy as it affects the less-developed countries.

McGeorge Bundy
President, Ford Foundation

Preface

The Energy Policy Project was initiated by the Ford Foundation in 1971 to explore alternative national energy policies. This book, *Energy And Agriculture In The Third World,* is one of the series of studies commissioned by the Project. It represents a pioneering analysis of the vital linkage between food and energy and is presented here as a carefully prepared contribution by the authors to today's public discussion of hunger in the underdeveloped countries.

It is our hope that each of the Project's special reports will stimulate further thinking and questioning in the specific areas it addresses. At the very most, however, each special report deals with only a piece of the energy puzzle; the Energy Policy Project's final report, *A Time To Choose: America's Energy Future,* which was published in October 1974, attempts to integrate these parts into a comprehensible whole, setting forth the energy policy options available to the United States as we see them.

This book, like the others in the series, has been reviewed by scholars and experts in the field not otherwise associated with the Project in order to be sure that differing points of view were considered. With each book in our series, we offer the opportunity of having their comments published, but none have chosen to do so with this volume.

Energy And Agriculture In The Third World is the author's report to the Ford Foundation's Energy Policy Project. Although neither the Foundation, its Energy Policy Project nor the Project's Advisory Board have assumed the role of passing judgement on the report's contents or conclusions, I certainly do commend it to all those who are seriously concerned with economic development in the poor nations of the world.

S. David Freeman
Director
Energy Policy Project

Acknowledgments

The consent and encouragement of Dave Freeman and the funding of the Ford Foundation enabled me to have the special privilege, as a staff member of the Energy Policy Project, to write this book. I thank them for it.

Alan Poole wrote the Appendix on biogasification and contributed extensively to the sections of biological energy sources in Chapter 4. His suggestions on many other matters were decisive; his enthusiasm for this book, insuppressible.

Francisco Otero did much of the background research for the prototypical villages of Chapter 2, particularly the Chinese, Tanzanian, Nigerian and Bolivian examples. I learned much about development economics from my discussions with Raj Krishna.

Dave Sheridan taught me a great deal about writing and helped to organize this book. Kitty Gillman edited it with skill, care and love. Taylor Vance, Shirley Cox and Billie Truesdell typed most of it and helped with the proof reading. Many other friends, among them Bob Williams, John Davidson, and Irene Gordon, made useful suggestions and kept me going with their encouragement and enthusiasm. And the reviewers of the first draft of this book made suggestions that proved very helpful when I revised it.

If this book has any inspiration, it was Annie Lepetit's rendition of Mozart's Phantansie in D minor (K-397) that provided it, for I often wrote as she played it.

Arjun Makhijani
Washington, D.C.
January, 1975

Energy and Agriculture in the Third World

Chapter One

Poverty, Agriculture, Energy

Wood is the poor man's oil. Throughout the underdeveloped world, men, women, and children spend a considerable portion of their time cutting trees, gathering twigs and branches, and tending fires to have the energy they need for cooking and a modicum of heat and light. Together with wood, animal dung and crop residues, human and animal labor provide the barest of energy necessities for 50 to 60 percent of the world's people who live in the villages and small towns of Asia, Africa, and Latin America.

The amount of energy so used is large—probably comparable to the flow of crude oil in the international market (about 30 million barrels a day). The commonly held notion that energy use in the underdeveloped countries is far below that in the industrialized nations[1,2,3] is based only on the use of "commercial" fuels, such as oil, coal and hydropower. The energy characteristic that is typical of poverty is not so much low per capita energy use—though that is part of it—but the relatively small amount of *useful work* that is obtained from it.

The full possibilities of the traditional fuels that poor rural people use are commonly slighted or forgotten. This study does not propose exclusive or even primary reliance on noncommercial energy sources for Third World development, but it does give them special attention because they have so often been neglected. When commercial fertilizer is scarce and fuel prices fearfully high, as they were in early 1975 when this book was written, the production of energy from small-scale, decentralized, noncommercial sources takes on extra importance.

This book seeks to explore how energy, in whatever form, may best help to transform agriculture, raise enough food, and provide other necessities for the people of the Third World, and to assess how much energy is needed to do this. But we must emphasize at the outset that energy alone is not enough. It is also imperative to move on many other fronts at the same time. Enough food

1

must be available to begin with to keep farmworkers alive and able to work. Other essential parts of the mosaic are medical care; land reform; technical assistance; loans for small farmers; birth control information and services; and a social system which assures that all the people, not just a privileged few, share in the fruits of development.

There is no question that more useful work, obtained both from more energy and more efficient use of energy, is essential to the development that must take place. In many poor countries arable land is limited. Energy helps to increase the yield that each unit of land can put forth—by working pumps for irrigation, by plowing fields, by harvesting crops, by producing fertilizer. In providing the energy, the pumps, the fertilizers, the cement needed to produce more food, poor countries burdened by shortages of capital and high food, oil and fertilizer prices, must make the fullest possible use of their resources.

Energy use in both agriculture and industry enables human labor to be more productive. Thus in the United States, about 10 percent of the work force, or less than 10 million workers in agriculture (including those engaged in the supply of fertilizers, tractors, and so on to farmers), supply enough food for the 210 million people in the U.S., with enough left over for substantial exports to other countries.[4] In many poor countries, 70 to 80 percent of the labor force are engaged in agriculture.

Increasing the productivity of land and labor—for which energy is essential—is, and has been, the foundation of economic growth.* How the wealth which flows from rising productivity of land and labor is parcelled out, both within nations and globally among nations, is of utmost importance. The long exploitation of poor countries' natural resources by industrialized nations (only recently reversed in the case of oil), the centuries-long exploitation of slaves in Europe and America, the great wealth of a few and the poverty of many in underdeveloped countries today—all illustrate that wealth among nations and within nations can increase, yet poverty and misery remain.

Economic growth, or the increase of a nation's wealth, does not automatically result in economic development. Such growth is an essential, but not a sufficient, condition for the people of a nation to achieve well being. The "Brazilian economic miracle" is a good example. Brazil's Gross National Product (GNP) grew at an annual compounded growth rate of 6 percent between 1960 and 1970. Despite this growth there were more poor people in Brazil in 1970 than there were in 1960.

Table 1–1 shows that fully 80 percent of the Brazilian people were

---

*Of course, there are other sources of national wealth, a most important one being the ownership of valuable natural resources. As the sudden wealth of oil-exporting countries shows, the sale of these resources can provide both ample income and capital for economic growth. Yet this wealth, which the high price of oil has transferred from oil-consuming to oil-producing countries, fundamentally rests upon the ability of industrialized nations to *use* the oil to achieve high productivity of land and labor.

Table 1-1.   Income Distribution in Brazil by Sectors of
the Population

	Percentage of the National Income		*Average Income per Capita (U.S. $)*	
Income Groups	*1960*	*1970*	*1960*	*1970*
Bottom 40%	11.2	9.0	84	90
Next 40%	34.2	27.8	257	278
Next 15%	27.0	27.0	540	720
Top 5%	27.4	36.3	1,635	2,940
Average			300	400

Source: Note 5.

hardly better off in 1970 than they were in 1960. The ranks of the poor (bottom 80 percent) increased from about 50 million in 1960 to about 65 million in 1970. Yet there are no indications of change in the economic policies that have brought wealth only to the rich, both in Brazil and in the industrialized nations (particularly the U.S. through the repatriation of the profits of the multinational corporations[6]).

This experience is not peculiar to Brazil. It is rather the rule in underdeveloped countries that the richest 5 to 15 percent are generally the ones to benefit the most from economic growth. They acquire automobiles, six-lane bridges, airplanes, and high-rise buildings on which precious cement and steel are wasted: stark monuments to the food, fertilizer and irrigation pumps that never were. Meanwhile the poor die from hunger and exposure.

Yet, the ones who die quickly may be the more fortunate, for the ones who survive live in misery. The most devastating by-product of poverty is the chronic malnutrition that afflicts hundreds of millions of people in the Third World. Children suffer brain damage from the lack of sufficient protein. Night blindness and total blindness afflict millions of others. These are the realities embedded in abstractions such as average income or GNP.

Redistribution of income is a fundamental reform to alleviate poverty. The redirection of capital spending to improve food production, land reform, health care, housing and provision of productive jobs for the poor are essential aspects of an income redistribution policy. In the People's Republic of China* such reforms have been a principal instrument in promoting the health and welfare of its people. The per capita availability of food in 1970 was about the same as it was in 1950,[7] and only slightly larger than the per capita food availability in India in 1970.[8] Yet, there is ample evidence to suggest that the

*Throughout this book the People's Republic of China is referred to as China. The Republic of China is referred to as Taiwan.

hunger and chronic malnutrition that afflict more than a 100 million people in India have been largely overcome in China. The equitable distribution of food and the widespread availability of medical care in China are among the principal reasons for the difference.[9]

Equitable distribution of the available food takes on even more urgent importance in this time of food and fertilizer shortages and cruelly high prices of food, fertilizers, and oil. These high prices not only make the severe balance of payments problems intolerable for the poorest among the oil- and food-importing countries,[11] but in these countries, as indeed in many others, the poor—particularly the urban poor and the landless rural poor—will bear the brunt of the food shortages. Poor weather in the Midwestern United States in 1974 resulted in a substantially lower crop production than anticipated; many fear that the food crisis will worsen. With these omens of world food shortages, increasing food production must be the primary goal of the underdeveloped nations if the future is to hold any hope for the poor. Agriculture and the activities that support agriculture must take precedence over all others for development in the poor countries of the Third World; they must have first call on available resources, energy included.

In this effort industrialization is essential. Industrialization is not and cannot be allowed to become the province of the wealthy nations, or of the wealthy people in the underdeveloped countries. Some essential industries, such as steel production or electric power generation, will remain capital-intensive in spite of every effort to reduce capital costs. Here it is of paramount importance that capacity be used as fully as possible and that the *output of these industries be used to create jobs and contribute to the rapid expansion of the production of essentials.* The primary aim of industrialization should be the same as that of aggressive promotion of agriculture—that of increasing the production of essential commodities, particularly food, as rapidly as possible, while ensuring that with the capital available, the creation of productive jobs stays well ahead of the growth of the labor force.

The technologies adopted for many industries are all too often imported wholesale from the industrialized nations without adequate consideration of alternatives that might be more suited to the capital-short economies of poor countries.[10] The kinds of technology that are used and the mix of industries that is established must suit each country's own natural capital and labor resources. In poor countries, the mix of industries must be determined by the most pressing needs of their people—that is, the production of food, clean domestic water supply, clothing, and housing.

One of the most tragic results of the failure of past development efforts to provide enough productive jobs has been the enormous waste of human resources. In stagnating village economies ... In the streets and slums of the cities to which some 20 million people find their way each year in the futile hope of an escape from the poverty of the villages.[11] If the grim prospects implied by high-population and labor-force growth rates are to be averted, it is imperative that development strategy be redericted to achieve both economic growth *and* employment objectives.[12] In most underdeveloped countries, the jobs must be created in agriculture. Gunnar Myrdal, in his study of poverty in South Asia, said, "The hope, so commonly expressed, that a large proportion of those who will join the labor force in the decades to come will become productively employed outside agriculture is illusory."[13]

In India, for example, the labor force will grow from the present 225 million to about 400 million in the next 25 years. Even if industrial employment grows at 5 percent per year (which means an optimistic 7 to 8 percent growth rate for industry[14]), only 25 to 30 million workers will be employed in industry by the turn of the century. Thus, in the next 25 years, about 100 million jobs must be created in the rural areas, which today are 80 percent dependent on agriculture. This must be done even while existing and new jobs are made much more productive so that the poor can move rapidly beyond a hand-to-mouth existence. This is an enormous task, especially since most of the cultivable land is already being used. The solution clearly points toward labor-intensive technologies[15,16,17] and an intensified use of agricultural land.[18]

Labor-intensive technologies are also essential because even the best efforts at birth control cannot now avert the large increase in the labor force in the next 15 to 20 years. These potential workers have already been born, and many more will be added in this decade.

Labor-intensive technologies, as we shall use the term in this book, are those which, in sum, result in *the most productive use of the entire pool of available labor,* with the capital that is available to a country. This has several major implications for investment in agriculture. First, it means the investment must be directed preferentially toward those areas, such as irrigation, that increase both labor productivity and employment.[19] Second, where mechanization in agriculture is essential to increase the productivity of land and labor but where it creates a net loss of jobs, then investment in other sectors of the economy, including public works, should take up the slack and productively absorb the displaced labor.[20,21] In some cases it may even be necessary to slow down the rate of mechanization of some farm activities such as threshing which cause a net loss of jobs, so that the poor may eat.[22] Third, the mix of technologies chosen for accomplishing a given increase in production should emphasize those which require a smaller amount of capital to create a given number of jobs. An example may serve to illustrate the principle.

Capital-intensive schemes of fertilizer production and electricity production for irrigation provide one job for every $20,000* of capital

*We have used the U.S. dollar as the unit of currency throughout this book. and the prevailing official exchange rates to convert various currencies to U.S. dollars. This use of dollars as a common currency measure, of course, does not imply foreign exchange costs or benefits.

investment (excluding the indirect employment effects due to increased agricultural output). Producing electricity and fertilizers in a village scale plant that uses animal dung and crop residues* can provide one job for every $3,000 of capital investment. The decentralized scheme provides more jobs because of the labor involved in collecting the dung and crop residues and operating the plant. For the most part, unskilled labor is required. In many places, this development scheme makes the labor that is already used in the husbanding of organic wastes more productive because the capital investment permits the use of the wastes for productive activities such as soil fertilization and irrigation (Chapter Four, Appendix B). Of course, this does not mean that chemical fertilizer factories should not be built. They should, for chemical fertilizers are essential to the progress of agriculture in the Third World (see discussion in Chapter Three). It does mean that the physical, monetary, and human resources available in each country should determine what mix of technologies is best suited to achieve given targets of food, fuel, or fertilizer production.

The abundance of human beings and domestic animals in the underdeveloped countries naturally raises the question: Why use fuels at all to supply mechanical energy? There are several important and fundamental reasons.

In agriculture, the foremost reason is to provide water for irrigation. The cheapest and quickest way to provide irrigation in many, if not most, areas of the world is to tap subterranean water sources (lift irrigation). Mechanical energy is practically a must for such irrigation. While human and animal labor can provide some water, as is common practice today, it cannot provide enough, even in the most densely populated agricultural regions such as the Indian Gangetic plain.

The high peak demand for labor which typifies nonmechanized agriculture[23,24,25,26] has two important deleterious effects. First, it is directly responsible for the dearth of jobs in rural areas for much of the year. Second, it probably encourages a high birth rate among farming families.

Mechanical power is essential both for the selective mechanization of those agricultural operations (such as threshing, rice transplantation, or harvesting) which make the heaviest peak labor demands,** and for irrigation. The use of human labor for irrigation is relatively unproductive. A penny's worth of electricity (at 5¢/kwhe) can provide as much water as a man at a hand pump all day.† Irrigation creates a very large demand for labor in the fields due

*Dung and crop residues can be converted to methane (a gaseous fuel akin to natural gas) by the action of anaerobic bacteria. The residue is high in nitrogen, phosphorous, and potassium, and can be used as a fertilizer. See Chapter Four and Appendix B.

**We cannot dismiss human and animal labor. As we shall see in Chapter Three, employment and income distribution effects are of paramount importance in the considerations of mechanization.

†Except for energy units, all units used in this book are metric. Energy is measured in Btu, which is the amount of energy needed to heat 1 pound (453.6 grams) of water by 1°F, and electricity in kilowatt hours electrical (kwhe). One kwhe = 3,413 Btu (excluding generation, transmission, and distribution losses). One barrel of oil = 42 U.S. gallons = 5.8 million Btu. One ton of coal = 1,000 kg of coal = 28 million Btu.

to increased crop production and multiple cropping.[27,28] Multiple cropping (growing more than one crop each year) exploits the abundance of year-round solar energy that is available in most underdeveloped countries, but irrigation is generally required for it, particularly in monsoon areas where the rainfall is concentrated in a few months of the year.

Mechanized irrigation can thus increase both employment and production substantially. But mechanized irrigation requires mechanical power, and it is here that the role of energy in agriculture, particularly in the forms of electricity, oil or gas, is most crucial in raising the productivity of farms and labor, while providing the job opportunities essential to any equitable distribution of the fruits of economic growth.

The data in Table 1–2 show that labor productivity and employment can be complementary when irrigation and fertilizers are available. Significantly, Japan, by far the most industrialized nation among those listed, has both the highest input of labor and the highest farm productivity, despite the widespread use of small tractors there. In subsequent chapters, we shall investigate in more detail the use of energy for irrigation and in other areas where it is important to agricultural development and, hence, to economic growth.

Just as labor is abundant in underdeveloped countries, so is capital scarce. This shortage of capital is at the root of many of the frustrations of development efforts. Obviously it is difficult to increase savings in underdeveloped countries where the economy is barely at subsistence level; most people find it hard to save for a better tomorrow when it requires all their effort to stay alive today.

A technology which can get more useful work out of energy with a modest capital outlay is clearly the best of bargains for poor countries. As we shall show in Chapter Four, decentralized village plants can, in the right circumstances, equal the fuel and fertilizer output of centralized systems at half the capital cost.

Another test for the effective employment of capital is the capital-output ratio. The rate of growth of all economies, and particularly those of the underdeveloped countries which are short of capital, depends critically on the annual production that can be obtained from the investment of the available capital. If the capital needed to increase annual production by a given amount is reduced (that is, if the incremental capital-output ratio* is lowered), the effect is the same as if more investment capital were made available. We shall show that agricultural development projects based on tubewell irrigation and on the use of crop residues and animal wastes to provide fertilizer for the fields and fuel for raising underground water can yield an annual output roughly twice the value of the capital required for the project—that is, a capital-output ratio of about one-half. (See Chapter Four for a full discussion). This is considerably less than

---

*In this book the term "capital-output ratio" refers to the incremental capital-output ratio—that is, the number of units of capital required to be added to present capital stock to increase annual production by one unit.

Table 1-2.   Employment and Labor Productivity in Rice Production

Country	Number of Workers per 100 Hectares (1965)	Labor Productivity Kilograms of Rice per Worker per Crop[a]	Land Productivity Kilograms of Rice per Hectare (1969)	Percentage of Rice-producing Land Irrigated[b]	Nitrogen Fertilizer Application Kilograms/Hectare[d] (1970)
Japan	215	2,600	5,600	100	~150
China	180–200	1,500	3,000	70	~50[c]
Taiwan	195	2,050	4,000	100	~100
India	90	1,550	1,400	40	~10 to 20

Sources: Notes 11, 15, 16.

[a]In Japan and Taiwan multiple cropping (three or four crops per year) is common, so that the annual productivity of the worker is several times his productivity per crop. Multiple cropping is less common in China and India.

[b]The percentage of irrigated area under rice cultivation is generally higher than national averages for all crops, because rice-producing areas are irrigated in preference to other crops.

[c]Includes the nitrogen content of organic fertilizers, which supply about 60 percent of the nitrogen.

[d]Nitrogen application is averaged over the entire area planted with rice. In practice, chemical nitrogen is applied to only part of the area. The average, therefore, indicates the extent of use rather than the typical practice in application of nitrogen per hectare.

Note: Throughout this book, the rice yield (kilograms of rice per hectare) is understood to mean the yield of unmilled rice (rice paddy) unless otherwise specified.

the capital-output ratio of 2.6 for agriculture in India's fifth five-year plan.[29] It is also much lower than India's average capital output ratio of 3.9 during the 1960–69 period.[30] Such a capital-output ratio can mean rapid economic growth, with agriculture providing the cutting edge of economic growth. This is another important reason for underdeveloped countries to focus their development efforts on agriculture.

Even with every effort to minimize the capital needed for economic development, procuring capital for investment from savings is a serious problem in most underdeveloped countries. India's entire development budget for almost 600 million people is considerably smaller than the expenditures of U.S. consumers on electric household appliances; it is about equal to sums spent on dogs, cats and other pets in U.S. homes. Public investments in the underdeveloped countries are often in the range of $10 to $20 per capita per year.

So long as development efforts continue to bypass the poor, the tax base will remain small and capital will remain scarce. But, there is no question that rural areas where the general level of living is rising can contribute significantly to capital formation in underdeveloped countries. In Japan, agriculture's contribution to the tax revenue in the late nineteenth century was around 85 percent;[31] this was the same period when Japan began to acquire the status of a major industrial power.

The capital contributions of farmers to agricultural development are substantial in several Asian countries. "In the late nineteen sixties deposits in the local [farm] cooperatives of Japan averaged 84 percent of the working capital [of the cooperatives]; in Taiwan 76 percent, in Korea 50 percent. In other Asian countries deposits amounted to only 1/10 or less of working capital."[32]

We cannot, however, expect the savings of farmers to increase much until their incomes begin to rise. Since commercial banks are usually unwilling to provide what they feel to be insecure loans to small farmers, the role of government in providing the capital necessary to initiate rural development is crucial. Without it the vicious circle wherein poverty limits savings and limited savings perpetuate poverty cannot be broken.

Development programs that focus their efforts on where the people are—the villages and small towns—are essential if the majority of the people in the Third World are to share both the labor and the fruits of economic growth. Such participation in economic development is also essential to the provision of adult education, health care, and birth control. Recent research in population growth rates and the practice of birth control in different nations shows that this feeling of participation and hope, and an equitable distribution of the fruits of economic growth, are strong forces in motivating smaller families. We quote at length from William Rich's recent report on birth control:

> There is, however, striking new evidence that in an increasing number of poor countries (as well as in some regions within

countries), birth rates have dropped sharply *despite* relatively low per capita income and *despite* the absence or relative newness of family planning programs. The examination of these cases in this monograph reveals a common factor. The countries in which this has happened are those in which the broadest spectrum of the population has shared in the economic and social benefits of significant national progress to a far greater degree than in most poor countries—or in most Western countries during their comparable periods of development. Family planning programs generally have been much more successful in those countries where increases in output of goods and social services have been distributed in such a way that they improved the way of life for a substantial majority of the population rather than just for a small minority.

The record also shows that those countries which continue to sustain high rates of population growth despite their achievement of relatively high per capita income figures have wide disparities in income and limited access to social services. Only a small group within these countries has started to practice fertility control; this group generally consists of the favored minority that has benefited most from the modern social and economic systems. The remainder of the society—those living at, or close to, the subsistence level—accounts for the high average birth rate.[33]

The People's Republic of China, which has emphasized agricultural production and equitable distribution of wealth, and in addition has created a unique decentralized health care system involving paramedical personnel as well as physicians, has experienced dramatic declines in the birth rate in recent years.[34]

We have argued that agriculture should be the focus of development efforts in most underdeveloped countries. As with any development planning, it is vital that the efforts be coordinated. Isolated efforts, such as electrification or birth control teams visiting villages, are insufficient for rapid progress because, in the struggle for survival, rural people have made many and complex adjustments to their harsh economic environment. Changes in any one factor are therefore not likely to be accepted or, if they are, will be inadequate for the cause of sustained economic progress. Experience with electricity use in Indian villages illustrates this point. An Indian government study found that growth of electricity use often stops, and that its use declines, 10 years after the introduction of electricity; at this point only about 20 percent of the population use electricity in agriculture, business, or industry.[35] This is clearly a symptom of economic stagnation, of equipment falling into disrepair and disuse, and probably of a lack of savings to replace worn-out equipment.

There are many reasons why simplistic solutions at rural development will not bring about the desired results. Among them are:

1. The problem of adequate nutrition so that people can work more vigorously is of great importance if we are to look to poor unemployed or underemployed labor as a significant contributor to economic growth.[36] The nutritionally unbalanced one meal a day to which so many poor people are constrained is wholly inadequate to sustain a vigorous work day.

2. Land reform, or at least consolidation of each family's land holdings, is essential to obtaining the full benefits of irrigation.[37] Scattered parcels of land cause a waste of labor and make farm and irrigation mechanization aimed at removing labor bottlenecks expensive and difficult.[38, 39]

3. Successful introduction of the high-yield crop varieties of the "Green Revolution" requires irrigation, fertilizers, pest control, agricultural extension services, and high-peak labor or selective mechanization simultaneously.

4. Working for and sharing the fruits of economic growth not only make progress real today but impart a feeling of hope and security for tomorrow that is essential to birth control programs[40] —and population stabilization is essential to the well-being of those already born and the children of the future.

The transformation of agriculture in the Third World requires much more than the development of individual village economies. The villages of the Third World are usually too small to support full-time agricultural extension workers, a hospital, a bank, servicing facilities for agricultural machinery, and so on. Most importantly, a prosperous agriculture requires organized markets to which farmers can bring and sell their surplus production; where they can purchase the consumer goods and services necessary to improve their lot, and the capital goods and services necessary to the economic health of their farms. The market town also serves as a focus for the diversification of the rural economy and a base for many small scale industries, such as bicycle manufacture or the production of leather goods.

The case for establishing market towns of a few thousand to 50,000 people to serve as a geographical focal point for developing the surrounding agriculture has often been persuasively argued.[41,42] The rates of increase of the population in large cities in the Third World are often 5 to 6 percent per year.[43] Horrendous projections of a Calcutta with 66 million people 25 years hence have not jogged the planners and governments to action, even though in today's Calcutta, with a tenth of that number, a million or more people live in the streets and slums, and jobs are hard to come by.

The number of market towns that must be established depends on such factors as population density and modes of transportation in common use. The average area served by such towns varies between 115 square kilometers in Taiwan to 450 square kilometers in Yugoslavia, with the speed of transportation being the principal constraint on the area served.[44,45] Here the building of roads, capital to finance the most effective means of transportation, and the fuel to power it are essential to the proper functioning of the market town.

Large-scale industrialization appropriate to larger towns and cities is necessary to support the development of agriculture. This is true in spite of the fact that an emphasis on labor-intensive technologies and an emphasis on local resources tends to make production of many goods economical at the scale of a village or market town plant. The failure of China's Great Leap Forward is a reminder that many industrial activities, such as steel production, are too expensive on a decentralized basis. Pumps, electric motors, and similar goods must be manufactured on a large scale or they will cost much more than imported equipment. Roads and railways must be built; ports must be developed; large-scale power plants must be built to serve industry. But the main aim of an industrialization program at all levels (village, market town, and city) must be the support of a dynamic agricultural economy—one that transforms today's halting progress, punctuated with famine, into genuine economic progress for the Third World.

Notes to Chapter One

1. *World Energy Supplies 1960–1970*, Statistical Papers, Series J, No. 15 (New York: United Nations, 1971).
2. A. B. Cambel et al., *Energy R&D and National Progress* (Washington, D.C.: U.S. Government Printing Office, 1965).
3. Nathaniel Guyol, *Energy in Perspective of Geography* (Englewood Cliffs, N.J.: Prentice Hall, 1971).
4. Katherine Gillman, "U.S. Energy Use in Historical Perspective," Special staff report of the Energy Policy Project of the Ford Foundation, New York, November 1973.
5. Jose Serra, *El Milagro Brasilero: Realidad o Mito* (Santiago de Chile: Quimantu, 1971).
6. Ronald Muller, "Poverty is the Product," *Foreign Policy* 13 (Winter 1973–74): 71–103.
7. Owen Dawson, *Communist China's Agriculture* (New York: Praeger, 1970).
8. *India 1971–72* (New Delhi: Government of India, 1972).
9. Victor Sidel and Ruth Sidel, "The Delivery of Medical Care in China," *Scientific American* 230 (April 1974): 1927.
10. Gunnar Myrdal, *Asian Drama* (New York: Pantheon, 1968).
11. Edgar Owens and Robert Shaw, *Development Reconsidered* (Lexington, Mass.: D.C. Heath and Company, 1972).
12. Raj Krishna, "A Model of the Unemployment Trap, with Policy Implications," in *Fiscal Measures for Employment Promotion in Developing Countries* (Geneva: International Labor Office, n.d.).
13. Myrdal, *Asian Drama*, p. 1242.
14. Raj Krishna, "Unemployment in India," *Indian Journal of Agricultural Economics* 28 (January–March 1974).
15. Leslie Kuo, *The Technical Transformation of Communist China's Agriculture* (New York: Praeger, 1972).

16. *Production Yearbook 1972,* Vol. 26 (Rome: Food and Agriculture Organization of the United Nations, 1973).
17. Planning Commission, *Approach to the Fifth Plan* (New Delhi: Government of India, 1973).
18. Myrdal, *Asian Drama.*
19. Krishna, "Unemployment in India."
20. Myrdal, *Asian Drama.*
21. Krishna, "Unemployment in India."
22. Myrdal, *Asian Drama.*
23. Krishna, "Unemployment in India."
24. John Mellor et al., *Developing Rural India* (Bombay: Lalvani Publishers, 1972).
25. John Mellor, "Report on Technological Advance in Indian Agriculture as It Relates to the Distribution of Income," International Bank for Reconstruction and Development, December 1969.
26. Robert Shaw, "Jobs and Agricultural Development," Monograph No. 3 (Washington, D.C.: Overseas Development Council, 1970).
27. Krishna, "Unemployment in India."
28. Planning Commission, *Approach to the Fifth Plan.*
29. *Ibid.*
30. Owens and Shaw, *Development Reconsidered.*
31. *Ibid.*
32. Krishna, "Unemployment in India," p. 93.
33. William Rich, "Smaller Families Through Social and Economic Progress," Monograph No. 7 (Washington, D.C.: Overseas Development Council, 1973), pp. 2–3.
34. Sidel and Sidel, "The Delivery of Medical Care."
35. Planning Commission, *Report on Evaluation of Rural Electrification in India* (New Delhi: Government of India, 1965).
36. Myrdal, *Asian Drama,* p. 689.
37. *Ibid.*
38. Mellor et al., *Developing Rural India.*
39. Gilbert Etienne, *Studies in Indian Agriculture* (Berkeley: University of California Press, 1968).
40. Rich, "Smaller Families."
41. Krishna, "Unemployment in India."
42. L. K. Sen et al., *Planning Rural Growth Centers for Integrated Area Development* (Hyderabad, India: National Institute for Community Development, 1971).
43. Krishna, "Unemployment in India."
44. Rich, "Smaller Families."
45. National Council for Applied Economic Research, *Market Towns and Spatial Development in India* (New Delhi: NCAER, 1965).

Chapter Two

Vignettes of Third World Agriculture

The first essential in making development policy is to analyze how agriculture is practiced and how energy is used in rural areas in the Third World. Detailed country studies must underlie the creation of development plans. A more realistic assessment of rural resources than has been previously available is a fundamental requirement to set directions for research and to lay the basis for sound policy.

The kind of region-by-region, village-by-village studies that are needed do not yet exist. But some suggestive observations do emerge from a study of the scattered material which is available, including anthropological studies, rural surveys, and national and regional data on population, crop yields, land to man ratios, and so on.

In this chapter we first offer some general remarks about Third World energy and agriculture, drawn from the fragmentary data that exist. We then use a similar data base to construct six examples of rural village life in China, India, Tanzania, Nigeria, Mexico, and Bolivia. The chief reason we present composite prototype villages, rather than real places, is the lack of comprehensive local studies on the connections between energy and agriculture. But the composites do offer an advantage in that they provide typical views of their regions and show how life in the village relates to national and regional policy.

We use these prototypes not only to show how people live on farms and villages in the Third World at present but also, in succeeding chapters, to demonstrate possibilities for change. The aim is to show in concrete detail what potential for development may lie beneath the surface of these villages, despite the misery in which many of the villagers now exist.

Since the data used here are not definitive but only indicative, extrapolations should be made with caution. Conditions within a country or region, or even among nearby villages, may vary enormously Attempting due caution, inferences are made in order to build up a more or less complete picture of villages in diverse areas. Firewood use, fertilizer use, technologies and costs of electrification, extraction of water from subterranean sources, and so on, are deduced from regional trends and national statistics. Where basic data were lacking, energy use was inferred from data that do exist for similar circumstances in other countries. Even from the fragmentary information available, it is clear that the rational use of energy in agriculture is a cornerstone for development.

Before proceeding to detailed descriptions of villages and regions, some important but often little known facts about Third World agriculture need to be considered.

If the total amount of energy, including animal and human labor, which goes into farming is calculated, the results are surprising—farms in underdeveloped countries often use more energy per hectare than farms in the industrialized nations. It takes more energy to feed the bullocks and mules that work the fields of much of the Third World, than to farm with the heavily mechanized methods of U.S. agriculture. Since farms in the U.S. are generally much more productive per unit of land, energy use per ton of food in the underdeveloped countries is much higher in comparison with mechanized farming, even when the heavy energy investments in irrigation and fertilizers are taken into account.

The widely held notion that subsistence farming is more frugal than mechanized farming in its use of resources—particularly energy resources—is false. While today's mechanized farming uses more nonrenewable energy resources than subsistence farming and wastes the energy value of crop residues produced in the fields, there is no intrinsic reason why these abundant crop residues could not substitute for the oil used by farm machines (Chapter Four).

The idea that subsistence farming is harmless to the environment is another misapprehension. The spreading Sahara desert, as well as the soil erosion and flooding in South Asia, all of which are partially due to overgrazing and deforestation, bear witness to the heavy economic and ecological price that is paid when ancient agricultural practices, designed to support millions of people, are used to try to sustain billions of people and domestic animals.

Data on the energy intensity* of rice production in India, China, Taiwan, and the U.S. are shown in Table 2–1. A few conclusions can be drawn from this table.

The installed horsepower per hectare is highest in Japan and the U.S., but the energy required for farm operations (plowing, sowing, harvesting, etc.) is smaller in the U.S. than in other countries. In Japan energy use per hectare is moderately low.

Much of the horsepower on Third World farms is in the form of animals. For every hectare of cultivated land in India there is one draft animal,

---

*Energy intensity of farming is defined here as the amount of energy, including the indirect energy inputs in the form of fertilizers, that it takes to produce one ton of food.

Table 2-1. Energy Use per Hectare in Rice Production in Various Countries[a, b]

Country	Installed horsepower hp per ha[c] farm machines and draft animals[d] only	Energy for farm operations million Btu per ha[e]	Energy for irrigation and nitrogen fertilizers manufacture million Btu per ha	Total energy input per ha million Btu	Rice yield kg/ha	Energy intensity million Btu per ton of Rice
India	0.7	20	6.5	26.5	1,400	19
China	0.7	20	12	32	3,000	10.7
Taiwan	0.5	10	22	32	4,000	8
Japan	1.6	10	25	35	5,600	6.2
U.S.A.	1.5	7	25	32	5,100	6.3

Sources: See Chapter One, Table 1–2, and Appendix A; notes 1, 2, 3, 4, 5.

[a]We have chosen to compare a single grain (rice) since total grain production not only depends on seed variety, soil quality, etc., but also on the mix of grains grown. Comparing a single grain, therefore, gives a better comparison of the energy intensity of various farming methods. *The numbers in this table are very approximate.*

[b]Installed horsepower and energy use are based on national average energy use in agriculture. *The numbers in this table are very approximate.* For India and China about 20 percent of the installed horsepower is in tractors; for Taiwan 50 percent; for Japan 90 percent; for the U.S. 100 percent.

[c]For India and China about 20 percent of the installed horsepower is in tractors; for Taiwan 50 percent; for Japan 90 percent; for the U.S. 100 percent.

[d]We assume that one draft animal (ox, horse, mule) is approximately equal to ½ horsepower. This implies a draft animal of about 250 kg[3]. For lack of data, it is assumed that draft animal weight is about the same in all poor countries. *Since a bullock or horse weighing 250 kg. is a rather small animal, this assumption may give rise to an underestimate of installed horsepower for some countries (e.g., Taiwan).* It is assumed that 75 percent of the energy output of the draft animals is used on farms, the other 25 percent being used for transportation, pumping domestic water, and similar nonfarm activities (which are excluded from the calculations). *Installed horsepower numbers include tractors, but exclude irrigation equipment, trucks, and autos on farms.*

Annual energy input per draft animal is assumed to be 25 million Btu. Tractor fuel input 7 million Btu/ha/yr for fully mechanized farms (U.S. data).

[e]The energy for irrigation varies according to the irrigation method, terrain, rainfall, water table depth, etc. For the purposes of comparison we have used 15 million Btu of energy input (3 million Btu of useful work) per irrigated hectare per crop. Thus in India, about 40 percent of the rice-producing land is irrigated, so that the irrigation energy input per hectare of rice-producing land is taken as $0.4 \times 15 \times 10^6$ Btu or 6 million Btu. The energy input for chemical nitrogen fertilizer manufacture is about 75 million Btu per metric ton of nitrogen. No energy cost is assigned to the preparation of organic fertilizer. The energy requirements for potassium and phosphorous are small compared to those for nitrogen fertilizers.

usually a bullock. Much the same is true of most subsistence agricultural economies in Asia and Latin America. (In much of tropical Africa human labor predominates.) Draft animals are relatively inefficient sources of mechanical power (though they are not as inefficient when the dung is used effectively). This is particularly true of the illfed, weak draft animals common in India and Africa, since a greater share of the energy they consume goes toward the maintenance of their metabolism.

Of the five countries in Table 2–1, Japanese farms have the highest installed horsepower per hectare. If one adds the approximate horsepower requirements for irrigation* and for the manufacture of tractors and fertilizers, we find that the total installed horsepower is 2.5 to 3 hp per hectare for the U.S. and Japan, 1.5 to 2 hp for Taiwan, and 1 to 1.5 hp for China and India. These differences in total horsepower are relatively small. However, the capital requirements for irrigation and the manufacture of fertilizers are large. Investment in these areas is essential to dramatic increases in agricultural productivity, except in cases where a copious source of foreign exchange is available to import food and fertilizers.

To some extent the differences in installed horsepower are misleading because the various kinds of specialized equipment that are used on Japanese and U.S. farms often have their own engines attached and each engine is used for fewer hours per year than the bullocks, mules and horses of the poor countries The power requirements for improving farm productivity can be decreased substantially if the equipment is designed for multiple uses (Chapter Three).

Table 2–1 shows that the energy required per hectare is about the same in all countries when the energy requirements of irrigation and fertilizers are taken into account. Since the yield of rice is higher in Japan and the U.S., the energy requirements per ton of rice are much smaller than in India or China. Table 2–1 also shows that as the use of irrigation and fertilizers increases, the production per hectare rises, and the total energy requirements per ton of rice decrease rapidly.

The data on rice indicate that the productivity of land depends on the amount of useful energy put into the farm, both directly in the form of farm work and indirectly through the application of irrigation water and fertilizers. Appendix A describes in some detail how the efficiences of the various technologies of energy use are specified in order to derive a measure of "useful energy."

Outside of field work, the energy requirements of the Third World are met largely by the use of wood. In most underdeveoped countries, particularly in Asia and Africa, the use of fuelwood exceeds the combined use of all forms of commercial energy. Dung and crop residues are other important energy sources. When these energy sources are omitted, as they often are in both

---

*The horsepower requirements for irrigation vary a great deal. We use 1 hp per irrigated hectare for illustrative purposes. See Chapter III and Appendix A for details.

national and international energy accounts (with the major exception of India), serious misunderstandings of comparative energy use arise. In fact, in the underdeveloped countries, the use of "noncommercial" fuels (wood, dung, and so on)* is much larger than the use of "commercial" fuels—about 25 million Btu per capita per year for noncommercial energy compared to 10 million Btu per capita for commercial fuels. [6,7,8,9,10] Total per capita energy use in the underdeveloped countries is, therefore, 30 to 40 million Btu per year or about one fourth of what is typical in the industrialized nations and about one-tenth of the average U.S. use.**

Deprivation of the benefits that energy brings is very real in the Third World. But to improve economic conditions of rural peoples requires something in addition to a general increase in the level of energy consumption. An immediate and less expensive way of achieving more benefits from energy in many cases is to make more efficient use of present resources, including all the noncommercial energy resources, which are relied upon so heavily in the Third World.

The following pages describe six areas of the Third World and prototypical composite villages, the data for which have been compiled from national, regional, and local sources. These six villages represent the basic variations of agriculture in the Third World except for agriculture as practiced by nomadic peoples and the slash-and-burn agriculture still prevalent in some areas, such as some islands of Indonesia and the Philippines.

Farming conditions and practices as well as the energy sources and uses that are typical of the vast majority of farmers in the Third World, are represented in these case studies. The irrigated wheat farms of Arango, Mexico, which are ploughed largely with tractors and are planted with high-yielding varieties of wheat and corn, are essentially similar to many farms in Punjab in Northwest India. The organic manuring practices on the rice fields of Southern China are common in South India and Taiwan. The manual farming unassisted by cattle, irrigation, or machines in the Tanzanian village (Kilombero) is typical of many areas of tropical Africa A few of the facts that emerge from comparison of these regions and villages are:

1. Adequate power to work the fields either in the form of draft cattle or farm machines, irrigation, and the use of fertilizers (chemical and organic) play crucial roles in determining the wealth of agricultural communities. Except for the farms which are run only with manual labor, energy use per unit of land is high, but the amounts of useful work derived from the energy varies a great deal from one place to the next (see Appendix A). Crop yields appear to be correlated with the useful work derived from energy use rather than total energy use.

*In all cases, wood not used as a fuel is excluded.
**Per capita consumption of commercial fuels is generally higher in Latin America than in Asia or Africa. [11]

2. The yields of crops vary not only from place to place but also from one year to the next, particularly in unirrigated areas. Since these are precisely the areas where economic conditions are most precarious, inadequate rainfall often brings disaster. In years of adequate rainfall, there may be surplus grain production, but often a lack of good storage facilities prevents a buildup of sufficient reserves to get by in the leaner years.

3. The peak labor problem is a feature of most agricultural communities, affecting those most that rely solely on human and animal labor.

4. The unplanned use of wood as fuel is causing problems which in many areas are already severe and will become so in others if better management of wood resources is not instituted. In the Sahel region of Northern Africa it contributes to the inexorable southward advance of the Sahara and in the Indian Subcontinent to flooding in the Gangetic and Indus plains.* [12] Yet the enormous resources of wood, land, and sunshine that are available in many underdeveloped countries in Africa, Latin America, and Southeast Asia could, if effectively used, help promote agricultural and economic growth.

When we speak of waste or inefficiency, we do so in the national context. Individuals without capital resources have no choice but to burn wood or dung the way they do. Thus, while the individual may use his resources as efficiently as he can, the nation may still be wasting resources by neglecting opportunities.

The primary aim of the vignettes of regions and prototypical villages which follow is to portray energy use in the context of agricultural practices and regional realities. This is the background for an assessment of the energy needs of agriculture, a technical and economic evaluation of some sources of energy that could fulfill those needs, and a discussion of the implications for agricultural development policy. Table 2–2 shows a summary of energy use in the prototypical villages.

INDIA

Of India's population of 580 million, about 350 million live in small villages of less than 2,000 people each. Most of these people are too poor to buy adequate food, medical care, decent housing, and sanitation, and the technological tools necessary to improve their productivity and income. A population growth rate of about 2.2 percent per year contributes to the monumental problems of economic and social development.

About 140 million hectares of India's area of 320 million hectares is cultivated land. [13] India therefore has a cultivated area comparable to that of the

---

*Extensive deforestation causes flooding because trees retard the flow of run of water into rivers and streams. Forests, therefore, not only help hold the soil together but they cause more of the rainwater to percolate to underground reservoirs. Trees, in effect, act as natural bunds in aiding soil conservation.

Table 2-2. Comparison of Energy Use in the Prototypical Villages[a]

| Place | Domestic Energy Use per Capita Million Btu/yr. | | Agricultural Energy Use Farm Work, Irrigation, Chemical Fertilizers in Million Btu/yr.[b] | | | | Energy Use per Capita in Transportation, Crop Processing and Other Activities Million Btu/yr.[b,d] | | Total per Capita Energy Use Million Btu/yr. | |
| | | | Per Capita | | Per Hectare[c] | | | | | |
	Useful Energy	Energy Input	Useful Energy	Energy Input	Useful Energy	Energy Input	Useful Energy	Energy Input	Useful Energy	Energy Input
1. Mangaon, India	0.2	4	0.5	7.7	1.6	25.6	0.1	3.4	0.8	14.7
2. Peipan, China	1	20	1.4	8.3	6.5	41.5	0.1	3.2	2.5	31.5
3. Kilombero, Tanzania	1.1	22	0.06	2.3	0.1	3.8	0.02	0.7	1.2	25
4. Batagawara, Nigeria	0.75	15	0.16	2.4	0.4	7.3	0.03	0.9	0.9	18.5
5. Arango, Mexico	1.6	17	13.5	41	14.9	45.5	0.1e	3.6e	15.2	61.6
6. Quebrada, Bolivia	1.7	33.3	0.3	6.7	1.8	40	0.3	6.6	2.3	46.6

[a]This table is derived from Tables 2-4, 2-8, 2-12, 2-15, 2-18, and 2-22.

[b]Half the human food has been included in the columns for agricultural energy use, the other half in the columns showing energy use for miscellaneous activities.

[c]The area of land which is cultivated (not including any multiple cropping) is used for computing energy use per hectare.

[d]Fifty percent of the human food and 25 percent of the draft animal energy is included in these columns, except for Quebrada, Bolivia, where 50 percent of the human food and 50 percent of the draft animal energy is included. For Kilombero, Tanzania, and Batagawara, Nigeria, we include only 25 percent of the human food in the "other" columns and 75 percent for farm work, because generally farm work is unassisted by draft animals or machines. The rest of the human food and draft animal energy is included in the columns showing agricultural energy use. This breakdown is somewhat arbitrary for we only know that most of the draft animal labor and a large portion of the human labor are used on the farms but have no empirical data on the subject.

[e]This number is probably an underestimate since we have not included oil or electricity for crop processing or oil for transportation of food and fertilizers.

U.S. or China, although its total land area is only about 40 percent as large as either country.

India's agricultural progress during the period 1950–1970 was substantial. Food (cereals and pulses) production doubled from about 51 million tons a year in 1950–51 to about 100 million tons in 1969–70, while population increased by about 50 percent. Thus, in spite of the severe drought of the mid sixties, the per capita availability of food increased. The average picture is, however, misleading because the distribution of this agricultural progress among the various regions of India as well as the distribution of the increased incomes from agricultural and economic growth has not been uniform. Thus Punjab (in Northwest India) has had spectacular growth in agricultural production and particularly in wheat production since the introduction of the high-yielding varieties of wheat in the late 1960s. Foodgrain production in Punjab increased at 15 percent per year (compounded) during the period 1966–70, and wheat production increased at 18 percent per year during this period.[14] Seventy-two percent of the cultivated area was irrigated in 1972, and about 40 percent of the cultivated area was sown more than once. Although all classes of farmers have benefited from agricultural growth, "the farmers in the higher income groups have gained relatively more than lower income groups," according to a sample survey in the Ludhiana district analyzed by Mohindar Mudahar.[15]

The regional disparities are even greater. Only 25 percent or so of India's cultivated land is irrigated, but in Bihar this figure falls to 10 percent [16, 17, 18] though Bihar lies on an amazingly rich source of subterranean water in the Gangetic plain which is recharged by many snowfed and rainfed rivers. Much of the irrigated area in India cannot support two crops a year because the water supply in many canal systems is insufficient. Many parts of India's irrigation system are quite old and were not built to cope with the intensive use required for high-yielding seeds and multiple cropping. Partly because of these inadequacies, only 20 percent of India's irrigated area is sown more than once a year.[19]

The picture is similar in rural electrification: 25 percent of the villages in India have electricity. In Haryana, in Northwest India, all villages have electricity; in Tamil Nadu the figure is 97 percent; in Punjab 55 percent; in Uttar Pradesh about 20 percent; in Bihar about 15 percent; and in Assam, in Eastern India, about 3 percent.[20, 21] The proportion of villagers who actually use the electricity where it is available is quite low. The rural electrification survey of 1965,[22] reported that electricity use in an average village ceases to grow when only 20 percent of the people use it.

While the lot of many rural people has improved since independence in 1947, particularly in the Northwest and in parts of the coastal plains, the lot of many of the landless and many farmers with small or marginal land holdings has not improved. In many cases it has become worse.

The food-fertilizer-oil crisis has hit India particularly hard. It was one of the principal factors in the decline in grain production from a high of 108 million tons in 1970–71 to 103 million tons in 1973–74. The trend of rising per capita food production in the 1950–1970 period was reversed in the 1970–74 period. Even in Punjab, India's most productive agricultural state, yields are declining because of a shortage of fertilizers and pesticides and lack of enough oil and electricity to run the irrigation pumps. At the same time the fertilizer plants of India are running far below capacity (50 to 60 percent).

India is one of the few countries where a systematic attempt has been made to determine the extent of use of noncommercial fuels. Sample surveys in villages and towns were conducted by the Energy Survey of India Committee to determine the extent of noncommercial fuel sources and uses.[23]

The Committee reported that about 120 million tons of wood, 50 million tons of dry dung, and 30 million tons of "vegetable wastes" were burned each year, largely in the villages but also in the towns. Vegetable wastes fed to draft animals were not considered in the report. If the energy taken in by draft animals is included, the per capita consumption of noncommerical energy is about 12 million Btu per year (about half of which is burned directly as a fuel) compared to the commercial energy use of 6 million Btu per year (about one-fourth of which is used to generate electricity).* About 10 percent of the commercial fuels are consumed in the villages primarily for irrigation and farm machines. The other 90 percent is consumed in the towns and cities, most of it going to industry and transport.

The statistics on noncommercial fuels are compiled in a way so that commercial fuels appear to play a larger role in energy use than is actually the case. If the energy content of both categories of fuel is measured on a Btu basis (or metric tons of coal equivalent), as is standard practice in almost all countries and in the United Nations, the noncommercial fuels assume more significance. With the international method of accounting, 86 percent of India's energy use in 1954–55 was in noncommercial fuels; with the "coal replacement" method used in India, the figure is about 70 percent.[16] For example, a metric ton of cow dung used for cooking is taken to be equivalent in energy value to the amount of coal that would replace it, if coal were used in place of the dung. Since the efficiency of coal burning is assumed to be higher, this practice understates the quantity of energy available in the dung. Energy in dung can be used just as efficiently as energy in coal, provided that it is burned in the right equipment. Therefore, the energy accounting procedure used in this book is based upon the energy content of the fuel. This gives us a more accurate picture of the amount of resources that are available and the amounts that are used.

Much of the world's poverty is concentrated in the rich alluvial plain of the Ganges River which consists of Bangladesh and the Indian States of Uttar Pradesh, Bihar, and West Bengal. The protypical village in Bihar that we have

*Fuel input for electricity generation is taken as 12,000 Btu per kwhe delivered, which is typical of many underdeveloped countries.[24]

chosen for study is poorer than villages in many other parts of India such as Punjab or the coastal areas of Tamil Nadu in South India. We have chosen it because it represents the conditions of life for a great many of the 300 million people who populate the Gangetic plain, and because we feel, that this area with its rich soil and water resources has great potential for agricultural growth. These are also among the reasons that we have used this village as the principal example in our illustrative calculations of energy needs and the economics of energy supply described in Chapters Three and Four.

Mangaon, India*

Mangaon, a village of 1,000 people, lies a few miles north of the Ganges River in Bihar—the heart of the Gangetic plain. Every inch of available land is cultivated here. The forests have long since been cleared, and the landscape is a patchwork quilt of small fields dotted with stands of fruit trees. Thirty percent of the people in Mangaon are landless, and another 40 percent of the families (five or six people per family) own less than one hectare scattered among many small holdings. The wealthiest 10 percent control almost half the land, and even these "wealthy" are usually poor; but they are the most powerful members of the community, controlling most of the credit and employing the landless who are usually indebted to them.

The average family holding is about 1.5 hectares (divided into many smaller plots), the median is about 0.8 hectares, and the land to man ratio is about 0.3 hectares per person. In many areas of Bihar, such as the Musahri Block, the ratio is much smaller—0.15 to 0.2 hectares per capita—and is falling rapidly under the severe pressure of population growth.

Governmental agricultural development programs are administered by the Block Development Officer. (A Development Block consists of 60,000 to 100,000 people.) Roads and wells are often as not put on property belonging to people with influence (often synonymous with bribing capability) rather than in places which would achieve the best result for the development of the area. There is a cooperative bank in the area, but the landless and many small landowners cannot take advantage of the low interest loans either because their holdings are too small and scattered to profit from them or they cannot offer the requisite collateral. They borrow from the money-lender (for buying seeds or food, for weddings, and so on) at annual rates of interest that are often run as high as 36 percent per year.[25] Development efforts have not been adequate to initiate rapid agricultural growth in this area. In Mangaon, which is representative of many poor villages of the Eastern Gangetic plain, the per capita availability of food has declined in the last 20 years, in contrast to the average statistics for India.

---

*The primary sources for the statistics are *The Musahri Plan* and *India 1971–1972,* notes 18 and 13, respectively.

Geography. Northern Bihar is crisscrossed by innumerable snowfed and rainfed rivers which often cause floods during the summer monsoon season. The Gandak River, which originates in Nepal, passes near Mangaon. The rainfall averages 100 centimeters a year, but can vary by a factor of more than two from year to year.[26] But because of the plentiful flow from the Himalayan rivers, there is an ample supply of water beneath the fertile alluvial soil. The subterranean water system and the rivers that crisscross the Gangetic plain are one of India's great agricultural resources. Sandy, loamy, and light clayey soils are most prevalent.

Farming Conditions and Practices. Despite a bounteous supply of subterranean water—the water table is often as little as 3 meters below the ground surface—and a snowfed river only a few miles away, only 10 percent of Mangaon's 300 hectares are irrigated. The irrigation system consists primarily of wells powered by draft animals, and irrigation water is used primarily to supplement rain water.

The inadequacy of irrigation and water control is a principal reason for poor yield on Mangaon's farms and therefore for the poverty of its people. The rainfall must be just right or there will either be drought or floods.* In one decade (1951–1960) there were two flood years and one year of severe drought. Deforestation in the hill areas to the South and on the North Gangetic plains appears to have played a major role in the increasing frequency of floods on both the Indus and Gangetic plains[28]. (Droughts are generally more damaging than floods for they can destroy a large proportion of the crop over vast areas). There have already been two droughts in the 1970s—in 1972 and again in 1974.

Drainage of water from the fields is a problem in the flat Gangetic plain. Building channels in the fields so that the extensive river system can be used for drainage increases the cost of providing adequate water control. However, canal irrigation in many areas has to be accompanied by a drainage system to supplement the natural drainage because canal irrigation is likely to cause an appreciable rise in the water table which is already close to the surface. Such increases in the ground water level that may damage the soil by waterlogging have, for example, been experienced in the Nagarjunasagar project in South India.[29]

The people and the 300 draft cattle provide almost all the labor for the fields, including the energy required to provide water for the 30 irrigated hectares. Table 2–3 shows the livestock data for Mangaon. Chemical fertilizers are not in widespread use, and neither are high-yielding varieties of wheat or rice, since irrigation is a prerequisite for their effective use.

---

*The Irrigation and Power Ministry of the central government has launched a major study of water resource development in the Gangetic plain, including flood control.[27]

Table 2-3.   Livestock in Managaon

Type	Number per Capita	Total
Draft cattle	0.3	300
Milch cattle	0.1	100
Horses, donkeys, mules	0.005	5
Goats and sheep		
(primarily goats)	0.8	800
Pigs	0.008	8

Energy.   Fuel cakes made of cowdung mixed with crop residues provide the main source of fuel. Cooking is the main fuel use, although several times each year the village potter buys several tons of cowdung with which to fire his kiln. After the surgarcane is harvested, substantial quantities of bagasse (cane residue after the juice has been extracted) are used as fuel to boil off the water in the cane juice to make raw sugar. Some wood is also used for cooking, but its use is not as large as in other parts of India because there aren't many trees. The ownership rights of trees are carefully defined since they are scarce.

Most of the crop residues are fed to the animals in quantities carefully calculated by long experience, so that a maximum benefit can be obtained from the scarce food available for the cattle (Chapter Three). Mangaon has no electricity. A few of the wealthier households have kerosene lamps, but the most common light is the dim glow of the hookah in the *baithak* (sitting place). Domestic water is obtained from wells and this task together with cooking and fuel collection occupies a large portion of the time of the women in Mangaon.

Table 2–4 summarizes the energy use in Mangaon.

Agricultural Production.   Rice is the main crop and is grown on the clayey soil in the wet season. The sandy soil is usually cultivated in the winter (*rabi* crop). Wheat, maize, and barley are the principal *rabi* crops. Sugarcane, gram, chillies, and potatoes are also grown. The rice yields are poor—often as low as 650 kg./ha. and average about 900 kg./ha. The all-India average rice yield is about 1,400 kg./ha. The yields of other crops are also usually below the averages for the rest of the country, which in turn are poor by the standards of the yields obtained in, say, Arango, Mexico, or the U.S.A. or the irrigated regions of Punjab and Haryana in India. Table 2–5 shows the yields and crop production in Mangaon.

Although there are a number of rivers in the vicinity, fishing is not a major activity. This is in contrast to West Bengal farther down the Gangetic plain. Systematic exploitation of the excellent opportunities for fishery development could provide a desperately needed source of protein to the people of the Gangetic plain.[30]

Table 2-4. Energy Use in Mangaon, India (Energy in Billion (10^9) Btu per Year Except Row 13)

Energy Source	Useful Energy	Efficiency Percentage	Gross Energy Input
1. Animal labor (including irrigation)	0.38	5	7.5
2. Woodfuel	0.05	5	1
3. Crop residues ⎫ direct use as fuel	0.05	5	1
4. Dung ⎭	0.1	5	2
5. Subtotal: noncommercial	0.6	5	11.5
6. Coal, oil (household use)	small	–	small
7. Electricity	–	–	–
8. Subtotal:commercial	small	–	small
9. Total: 5 + 8	0.6	5	11.5
10. Human energy	0.08	2.5	3
11. Chemical fertilizers	0.15	–	0.15
12. Total energy use: 9 + 10 + 11	0.8	5	14.7
13. Per capita energy use per year	0.8 million Btu	5	14.7 million Btu

1. Throughout the energy calculations in this chapter we assume that one bullock or horse produces a power of about ½ hp and works for about 1,000 hours per year (notes 1 and 3), yielding a net annual output of energy of about 1.2 million Btu. Input per draft animal is taken as 25 million Btu/yr. For human labor we assume a net energy output of 0.17 million Btu per year (50 kwh) for each person over 15 years of age. Daily intake of food is assumed 8,000 Btu (1 kcal = 4 Btu). Gross energy in human food includes food intake by all people.

2. The use of 5 percent efficiency for draft animals is discussed in Appendix A.

3. We have assumed an efficiency of 5 percent for the use of noncommercial fuels (wood, dung, and crop residues) by comparing energy used for cooking in gas stoves with that used in open cooking fires. The annual energy use in a gas stove without pilot lights is between 4 and 8 million Btu in the U.S., while the cooking energy requirements for a family using noncommercial fuels (without efficient ovens or stoves) is 20 to 30 million Btu per year. If we assign an efficiency of 20 percent to gas stoves—somewhat arbitrarily—then the efficiency of rural cooking would be about 5 percent. One of the main reasons for using measures of efficiency of energy use for domestic purposes is to get some idea of the potential energy surplus if rural energy sources are used more efficiently.

4. We assume that 75 percent of the animal labor and 50 percent of the human labor is for farm work.

Table 2-5. Annual Crop Production in Mangaon

Crop	Yield kg/ha	Area ha	Production tons
Rice	850	140	120
Wheat	850	30	25
Maize	1,100	50	55
Barley	850	30	25
Sugarcane	30,000	12	360
Pulses, vegetables, etc.	Variable	20	?
Fish			0.1

THE PEOPLE'S REPUBLIC OF CHINA*

China's 800 million people and their leaders have gained the admiration of the world for their progress in providing food, housing, and decent medical care for their people. This has been achieved because the Chinese have made equitable redistribution of income between city and countryside and agricultural production the pillars of their economic policy. More equitable distribution of food, achieved primarily through China's revolution in land ownership in which most of the land is communally owned and the rest shared among rural families, has been particularly important because China's agricultural growth has been very uneven. In fact, the overall growth in agricultural production in the 1950–1970 period barely kept up with population growth, and per capita food availability was actually lower in the late sixties than it was in the early thirties.[31,32]

Two of the principal causes for China's failure to achieve a sustained growth in per capita food production are related to the issues of energy and mechanization. The first, and probably more important, was that population growth was encouraged in the fifties and sixties; the second was the failure of the industrialization policy of the Great Leap Forward.

Mao Tse-Tung was a forceful advocate of increasing China's population.[34] While part of this advocacy may have been related to ideology, one reason appears to have been that China's policy makers perceived a shortage of labor.[35] They were only partially right. In China, as elsewhere in the Third World, agricultural innovation is often limited by the availability of labor at certain times during the crop cycle. The solution that China adopted was to encourage population growth and to try to even out the peaks in labor demand by multiple cropping, public works projects, and decentralized industries. While China has had considerable success with multiple cropping and decentralized industries (including rural electrification[36]), the failure of the population policy is clear—per capita food production did not increase between 1950 and 1970.

The failure of the Great Leap Forward was also related to the peak labor problem. By encouraging "backyard furnaces" to exploit local mineral deposits (iron in particular), not enough labor was available in the fields at critical periods. Development priority was changed from agriculture to heavy industry (both centralized and decentralized).[37] As the peasants found out in the famine that followed, they were damned if they worked the backyard furnaces and damned if they didn't.

It appears that these failures were related to the failure to properly analyze the nature of the peak labor problems. The Chinese have traditionally

*The principal reference for the economic policy discussion is Goodstadt's *China Search for Plenty* (note 33).

relied heavily on human labor, even for irrigation.[38] This tradition, reinforced by Marxist economics, was reflected in Mao's emphasis on human labor even while he was in favor of farm mechanization.[39]

The mistake of the Chinese planners was their failure to note that the peak labor problem was, in essence, an energy problem. Selective mechanization of peak labor operations with multiple cropping by using rice transplanting machines, harvesters, etc., would probably have been a more satisfactory solution than encouraging the production of babies who would consume food for at least 10 years before they could provide labor for the farms. This conclusion is reinforced by our earlier analysis (Table 2–1 of this chapter) that the use of animal and human labor creates larger energy demands per unit of food production than mechanized agriculture, and demands a much more precious form of energy—food.

That Chinese leaders have recognized these mistakes was evident in the mid-sixties during the Cultural Revolution and in the recent reversal of China's population policy.[40] The main emphasis of China's economic development policy today is agricultural development, as is illustrated by the fact the current heavy commitment to building chemical fertilizer plants.

Chinese farmers have traditionally husbanded organic wastes of all kinds for use as fertilizer.[41] Even today over half of China's nitrogen and perhaps 80 percent of the phosphorous and potassium fertilizers come from human and animal dung and vegetable sources.[42] To use the wastes as fertilizer the Chinese compost them and in so doing waste their fuel potential.

The use of coal and electricity for powering irrigation pumps and of oil for tractors (usually 15 horsepower) is rising rapidly, as is the use of chemical fertilizers. China currently exports about 30 million barrels of oil a year, and its oil production is expected to rise rapidly. Ninety percent of China's 10 quadrillion (10^{15}) Btu of commercial energy comes from coal.[43]

China has large surface and subsurface supplies of water for irrigation and the irrigated acreage has expanded rapidly.

Dawson[44] details a considerable controversy as to the "effectiveness" of the irrigation schemes. He cites a conservative estimate for 1967 of 39 million irrigated hectares—or 35 percent of China's cultivated land. On this basis the current (1974) "effectively" irrigated area would be about 50 percent, but 70 percent of the cultivated area would have some irrigation water available. The figure of 70 percent can be compared with India's 25 percent irrigated area, for in both cases the figures do not reflect the adequacy of the irrigation system to supply the quantities of water needed when it is needed.

China has a land area of about 950 million hectares (slightly more than the U.S.), but of this only about 150 million hectares are arable land, of which 110 million hectares are cultivated. This cultivated area is similar to that of India or the U.S. But since the potential for expansion at least in the next decade or two is not large, China must rely on increasing crop yields and on multiple cropping to feed its people. Currently China produces about 2 tons of grain per cultivated hectare per year which is intermediate between India (less than 1 ton/ha) and the U.S. (3 to 4 ton/ha).

Fish provides an important source of protein for the Chinese people. China is one of the largest fishing communities of the world, with an annual catch of about 10 million tons (extrapolated from Dawson[46]). One-third to one-half of the catch is from fresh water and marine farms. Chinese planners have been aware of the immense advantages in producing fish from such farms.

Energy. Wood is China's principal domestic fuel in rural areas. According to Richardson,[47] there exist no reliable estimates of rural fuel wood consumption. However, the physical evidence points to extensive use of wood and other vegetable matter as fuel as illustrated by the following quotes from Richardson's book, *Forestry in Communist China:*

> Another factor which may well contribute to the devastated appearance of young plantations is the very real fuel shortage in most parts of China. The great majority of rural Chinese must rely on wood and other vegetable matter for all cooking and heating purposes and, in the deforested areas (where 98 percent of the population is located), fuel is at a premium. In the rural communes, peasants are allowed to harvest dead trees for burning and they have, thus, a vested interest in early mortality. To tend trees for posterity, while freezing in the present from lack of firewood, demands an altruism scarcely to be expected, even in China; there is evidence, in fact, that, as happens in the new territories of Hong Kong, trees are stolen for fuel almost as soon as they have been planted.[48]
>
> No forest areas are maintained specifically for fuel in China and the bulk of the requirement is satisfied by loppings of branches, dead trees, and debris from the forest floor. As of right, peasants can remove dead trees from forests and plantations and can prune dead branches at two-year intervals. These practices have serious implications for plantation management, in that the people have a vested interest in early mortality of newly planted trees and, also, they disfigure established trees by reckless pruning. Mutilated and unsightly saplings, even in the forest-rich areas of Manchuria, bear witness to the widespread nature of these practices.[49]

However, if the use of wood as a domestic fuel in other countries is an indication, the use of wood and other vegetable matter in rural areas is probably over one ton per capita per year, taking into account that much of China has a temperate climate and is quite cold in the winter. This would amount to a total of more than 500 million tons annually. As in India and elsewhere, wood use is aggravating already serious soil erosion problems, particularly in hilly areas.[50, 51] The Chinese have active large-scale reforestation programs that have met with some success, but as the quotes above indicate, reforestation would be better served if a fuel wood plantation program were undertaken.

PEIPAN, THE PEOPLE'S REPUBLIC OF CHINA*

Peipan is a village located near the Tzu River in hilly Eastern Hunan. It is a village of about 1,000 people (200 households) which has a cultivated area of 200 hectares. Peipan is part of a commune of several villages which is the basic administrative unit for the implementation of national agricultural policy. The land in the commune is owned collectively by its members, but a small amount is privately owned. The annual and long-term production goals for the commune are set by the central government, but in its day-to-day operations are locally controlled. Decisions regarding the division of labor, production, and construction schedules are made at meetings presided over by Communist Party cadrés.

In spite of the idealogical campaigns, the influence of the clan in Peipan is still strong. However, the apathy to increasing production, which was a feature of Chinese village life before the revolution, has largely been overcome. One of the instruments of this change has been the grant of small private plots to each family for raising pigs and cultivating vegetables and bamboo or fruit trees in their spare time. They barter or sell the produce at local markets.

While the existence of private plots has at times been ideologically unpalatable to the ultra-leftists of the Communist Party, the necessity for such production incentives has long been recognized (and fiercely debated) by the government as an instrument of pragmatic economic policy. Many political fortunes have been made and lost in this debate over material incentives. (Whether you won or lost depended not only what side you were on but also on the current economic and political climate.)

The produce of the commune is distributed among its members and exported to the cities. Some of the coarse grains are fed to the animals— particularly the pigs and poultry. The share of the workers is determined according to their work and productivity (the "work point" system). Most of the rest of the produce is exported to cities and towns. These exports provide the capital with which most agricultural development has been financed. Such economic self-reliance has been a major feature of Chinese agricultural development policy.

*The main references for the agricultural data are Dawson, Kuo, and the Food and Agriculture Organization's *Production Yearbook,* (notes 31, 32, and 5, respectively).

Geography

The region has a mild temperate climate and receives about 100 centimeters of yearly precipitation. A small portion of the production is often lost to spring floods; but major floods are rare due to the many flood control and water conservation projects that have been undertaken. Droughts also occur every few years, but the irrigation system in Peipan helps reduce the losses.

Farming Conditions and Practices

About 70 percent of Peipan's 200 hectares is irrigated land. The terrain being hilly, much of the land is terraced and is therefore fragmented into many small plots. Traditionally, animal labor was used for irrigation. In years of drought, it was common for the cattle population to decline substantially from overwork and undernourishment. Today, most of the irrigation and drainage is mechanized, using pumps powered by electricity, oil, and coal. Irrigation from ponds and tube wells generally provides an ample supply of water for rice, which is the main crop. Farm machinery increasingly complements the human and animal labor in the fields. A great deal of work is devoted to maintaining the terraces, in ensuring proper drainage, and in the collection and use of manure.

Partly as a result of the National Program for Agricultural Development, the population of draft animals increased by 4.3 percent a year from 1949 to 1959. While there is disagreement on the extent of the drop in livestock population during the Great Leap Forward, growth in the population of draft animals recovered in the mid-sixties. We have used data from Dawson[52] and the FAO *Production Yearbook*[53] to arrive at the estimates shown in Table 2–6.

Sixty percent of the nitrogen fertilizer and about 80 percent of the phosphorous and potassium fertilizers come from organic sources, principally animal dung and night soil. The rest is provided by chemical fertilizers, the production of which is expected to increase several fold in this decade. The total nitrogen used is 12 metric tons per year, which averages about 60 kg/hectare of cultivated land. The use of P_2O_5 and K_2O averages about 30 kg/hectare of

Table 2–6. Livestock in Peipan

	Per Capita	*Total*
1. Draft cattle	.15	150
2. Horses, donkeys, and mules	.03	30
3. Hogs	0.5	500
4. Sheep and goats	0.25	250
5. Poultry	0.6	600

Sources: Notes 5, 31.

cultivated land. Rice, being the favored crop, gets larger than average applications of manure and fertilizers.

This rate of fertilizer use is quite high and is comparable to that in many industrialized countries. That most of this fertilizer comes from organic sources reflects the remarkable and careful husbanding of organic manure that has characterized Chinese agriculture for centuries.

Energy

Wood is still the principal domestic fuel and is used for cooking and heating, but we have no reliable data on the quantities used. We estimate an annual per capita use of 1.5 metric tons of wood and other vegetable matter using data on domestic fuel use from other parts of the world where non-commercial energy sources supply most of the energy.

Though irrigation and field operations in Peipan are becoming progressively mechanized, human and animal labor still play a large role in the village economy, as evidenced by the large amount of human and animal powered equipment (Table 2–7). About 75 horsepower is available from the 150 draft animals which are utilized 100 to 120 work days a year, yielding a useful energy output of about 250 million Btu. Draft animals are used primarily for transportation, ploughing, and other fieldwork.

Irrigation is mechanically powered, partly by electricity and partly by coal- and oil-driven engines. Electricity use in rural China is about 10 kwhe per capita per year and is growing at about 10 percent per year. To accelerate rural electrification decentralized stations (500 kw) are used to complement the large-scale transmission and distribution systems.[54] A summary of energy use in Peipan is shown in Table 2–8.

Agricultural Production

Rice is by far the most important crop in this region. Corn, wheat, and soybeans are also grown, but they are not as important here as they are in Northern China. Potatoes and vegetables are staples grown almost solely for local consumption. Some coarse grains are fed to the pigs and cattle.

Table 2-7. Summary of Farm Equipment in Peipan

1 standard tractor (15 hp)
1 motor powered plough
1 motor powered harrow
50 horsepower of irrigation equipment
15 rubber wheel animal-driven carts
25 rubber wheel hand carts
An undetermined number of traces, yokes, ploughs, etc.

Table 2-8. Energy Use in Peipan (Energy in 10^9 Btu per Year Except Row 13)

Energy Source	Useful Energy 10^9 Btu/yr.	Efficiency Percentage	Gross Energy Input 10^9 Btu/yr.
1. Animal labor	0.25	5	5
2. Woodfuel			
3. Crop residues ⎱ direct use as fuel	1	5	20
4. Dung ⎰	—	—	—
5. Subtotal: noncommercial	1.25	5	25
6. Coal, oil (irrigation and farm machinery	0.6	20	3
7. Electricity			
8. Subtotal: commercial	0.6	—	3
9. Total: 5 + 8	1.85	6.5	28
10. Human energy	0.1	3	3
11. Chemical fertilizers	0.5	—	0.5
12. Total energy use: 9 + 10 + 11	2.45	7	31.5
13. Per capita energy use per year	2.45 million Btu	7	31.5 million Btu

Notes:
1. See Table 2-4.
2. Human food consumption taken as 8,000 Btu/day (2000 kcal/day). Useful work output per worker is taken as 200,000 Btu/yr.
3. Land cultivated per year—300 ha. Land irrigated—150 ha. (including double cropping).
4. Irrigation energy requirement (useful) is taken as 3 million Btu/ha/crop.

Crop yields vary depending on the region and the degree of implementation of the various parts of the National Plan for Agricultural Development. Table 2–9 shows figures which are probably typical of the Hunan region.

TROPICAL AFRICA*

Sub-Saharan Africa has a population of about 250 million people, and an enormous area of about 25 million square kilometers. Though it is rich in all manner of resources from land, sunshine and water to copper and diamonds, the problems of development here and the poverty of its people are as stark as one may find anywhere on earth. Here as many as a quarter of all the children die

*Mediterranean Africa (or Africa approximately north of the Tropic of Cancer) is not included in this discussion.

Table 2-9. Crop Production in Peipan

Crop	Summer Crop Yield kg/ha	Summer Crop Hectares Planted	Winter Crop Yield kg/ha	Winter Crop Hectares Planted	Total Annual Production Tons
1. Rice	3,000	100	3,000	50	450
2. Wheat	—	—	1,000	50	50
3. Potatoes	4,000	20	—	—	100
4. Corn, barley and miscellaneous grains	variable	50	—	—	100
5. Soybeans	1,100	10	—	—	11
6. Vegetables and fruits	variable	20	variable	?	?
7. Fish from ponds	?	?	?	?	3

Sources: Notes 5, 31, 32.

Note: Although we show two crops per year, "a triple cropping system of winter wheat, rice and coarse grain" (corn, barley, etc.) is often adopted in this region (note 31, p. 234).

before they are a year old. In remote rural areas as many as half the children die before they are 10 years old. The people are afflicted by all manner of diseases, caused principally by a combination of disease-bearing insects and malnutrition.[55]

Malnutrition here often takes the form of protein, vitamin, and trace mineral deficiency even though the availability of calories in the food sometimes exceeds the normal requirements. This is principally because of the predominance of cassava (2.4 percent protein content on a dry weight basis) and cereals in the diet of most people.

The economic, educational, and technical problems are difficult enough, but constant political strife both within and among the nations of Africa has been and remains one of the principal obstacles to development.

The tribal structure of African society, inflamed by divide-and-rule colonialists and the inflow of weapons from the industrialized nations, has, in many African nations, given rise to a political climate which is hostile to economic and social development. The colonialists, by imposing national boundaries that were convenient to them and arbitrary with respect to the history and realities of tribal Africa,[56] converted many independent tribes who fought occasionally, into nation states constantly at war within and with their neighbors. The nomadic Tuareg of Mali, striken by drought and disease, have, for example, been at the mercy of the politicians for years and have often suffered a policy of apathy to their needs. Many have fled to neighboring Niger. In Nigeria the Hausa and Ibo tribes fought a long and savage civil war; in Sudan Muslims are waging a bloody struggle for domination over various other ethnic groups; in South Africa and Zimbabwe (Rhodesia) white minorities continue to suppress the majority with aid, trade, and weapons from the West. (Interestingly South Africa is classified as a "developed" country by the United Nations in spite of the fact that most South Africans are poor.) Tribal frictions and conflicts abound in tropical Africa, and, in the words of D.F. Owen, are "doubtless a serious hindrance to economic development and political stability."[57]

Tanzania* is one of the few nations in tropical Africa where an attempt is being made to mold the traditions of African society into an effective means for the implementation of economic development policy. The concept of communal ownership of land, which was the typical form of land tenure in traditional tribal African society,[58] has become the basis for land reform and agricultural development. President Nyerere, who symbolizes Tanzania's unity, also represents the country's determination to increase agricultural production by spending a good portion of each year working in and visiting *Ujamaa* ("brotherhood") villages.

These *Ujamaa* villages, which are larger than the small isolated villages more usual in Africa, were established in order that basic services such as

*Much of the discussion on Tanzania is based on conversations with Tanzanian officials.

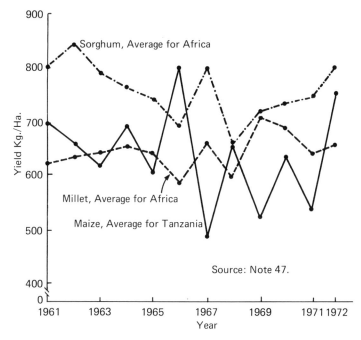

Figure 2-1. Annual Yield for Three Cereal Crops 1961-72.
Source: Reference 5.

clean potable water, agricultural extension, medical care, education, and transportation may be made available more easily and cheaply.

In spite of this ideological commitment and the fact that the Tanzania African National Union headed by President Nyerere has succeeded in keeping Tanzania relatively free of tribal tension (Nyerere himself comes from the small Zanaki tribe[59]), Tanzania's agricultural progress has been erratic. Although per capita food production has increased in the last 10 years or so*, the only consistent increase in both per hectare yield and total production for a major food crop has been in cassava,** a tuber practically devoid of protein. A glance at cereal production statistics for Tanzania and many other countries in tropical Africa reveals that yields vary enormously from year to year.

Figure 2–1 shows the large fluctuations in the yields of maize, millet, and sorghum, which are Africa's most important cereal crops. These yields have, on the average, not increased significantly in the past decade, although in some countries such as Kenya they have. Wheat and rice, which are

---

*It is not clear whether this observation holds for 1974 due to a drought in northern Tanzania.

**We have used the Food and Agriculture Organization's (FAO) *Production Yearbook* for most crop production and land use statistics in this section. It will not be cited further in this section.

the cereals next in importance in terms of acreage planted as well as production have shown fairly consistent improvement.

The lack of irrigation appears to be one of the principal reaons for Africa's slow progress in agriculture. In many countries less than 10 percent of the cultivated land* is irrigated. In 1965, Nigeria had only 13,000 hectares of irrigated land out of a cultivated area of about 21 million hectares. Generally speaking, the smallness of the irrigated area is not due to a lack of water resources except perhaps in the Sahel region and the Kalahari desert. The Zaire River at its peak has several times the flow of the Mississippi River; Lake Victoria in East Africa is one of the largest bodies of fresh water in the world. There are numerous other lakes and rivers and large stores of underground water (particularly in the Zaire, Zambezi, and Niger River basins[60]) which could be used to irrigate tropical Africa's farms. In hilly areas dams, tanks and gravity irrigation could provide reliable sources of water. A principal roadblock appears to be a lack of investment in agriculture.

Since the relatively large investments required for irrigation and the associated power facilities cannot be expected to come from farmers who live a hand-to-mouth existence, the schemes must be initiated by government investment. This is doubly true since the rich in underdeveloped countries prefer to live and to invest their money in the cities.

The provision of irrigation is only one of Africa's many agricultural development problems. Human, animal, and crop populations are regularly ravaged by disease bearing insects principal among which are the anopheles mosquito, various species of locust and grasshoppers, the tsetse fly, and many kinds of stemborers and plant suckers.** Overgrazing by cattle is another serious problem and contributes to the spread of deserts in many areas.[61]

The danger of isolated development efforts is well illustrated by the attempts to control sleeping sickness in cattle. These partially successful attempts have helped increase the rate of population growth among the cattle since there have been no serious attempts at simultaneously controlling their numbers. Thus the serious problems of the overgrazed savannah regions are further aggravated. It is D.F. Owen's view that under present conditions and development programs, sleeping sickness among cattle may, in the long run, turn out to have slowed the destruction of the savannah.[62]

Wood is Africa's principal fuel.† The extensive use of wood in the Sahel region is probably one of the causes of the spread of the Sahara desert. In countries like Gambia and Tanzania where wood is plentiful, current patterns of indiscriminate wood-cutting and its inefficient use may, in the long run, cause

---

*This includes land that is temporarily fallow. The land actually harvested in any year may be half to two-thirds of the total cultivated area.
**This short discussion of pests and cattle in Africa is based on D.F. Owen's book, Man in Tropical Africa.
†Statistics on wood use in Africa are based entirely on Openshaw's research in Gambia and Tanzania (see notes 6 and 7).

problems similar to the ones being experienced today by the countries in the Sahel region. *Yet the use of wood as an energy problem has received little attention either in national development efforts or in international assessments.*

Openshaw has compiled data on wood use in Gambia and Tanzania. While the bulk of the wood is only used for cooking and home heating, it is also used extensively in industry as fuel and timber, for water heating, for drying fish and cassava, etc. Per capita annual wood use amounts to about 1 metric ton (15 million Btu) in Gambia and 1.5 tons in Tanzania. Wood therefore supplies about 10 times more energy than all commercial fuels* in both Gambia and Tanzania.[63] It is instructive to note here that in Gambia the per capita use of energy for cooking in rural areas is 6 to 7 million Btu per year, a figure comparable to cooking energy use in rural India (about 5 million Btu). We shall use this fact in Chapter Three in analyzing the energy needs of rural areas.

In agriculture, human labor is the principal source of energy. In many parts of Tropical Africa, the introduction of draft animals is a revolutionary agricultural innovation. Crop yields in Africa are among the lowest in the world, partly because sufficient energy is not available to plough the land well, to weed thoroughly, or to harvest and thresh the grain. In Africa, as in other parts of the Third World, the peak labor problem is serious and probably encourages population growth. D.F. Owen has described the cultivation of rice in Gambia:

> Sickness and pregnancy are not regarded as excuses for not cultivating rice and all women who are remotely able to work are forced to do so.
>
> The concentration of heavy agricultural work into a restricted period of the year, together with seasonal changes in the availability of food, has a pronounced effect on the energy budget of the people. From March to May there is little or no work to do, the body weights of the people remain stationary, and their intake and expenditure of energy is low. With the onset of the rains heavy work commences and there is an increase in energy expended, which continues to increase as the rains develop and more and more heavy work becomes necessary. At this time of the year the store of food from the previous harvest is almost exhausted and a seasonal low of available energy is reached at the time when energy expenditure is greatest. This deficit results in a fall in body weight as the tissues of the body are drawn upon. Weight is regained at the beginning of the dry season when food from the harvest becomes available.[64]

These facts again illustrate how wasteful subsistence agriculture is of human and physical resources, and the crucial role that a proper understanding of energy flows must play in planning agricultural development.

---

*To be consistent in nomenclature, we do not include wood as a commercial fuel here. In practice it is one of the main sources of energy even in the cities where it is sold for 25¢ per million Btu as wood and about $1.50/million Btu as charcoal.

The consumption of commercial energy in tropical Africa averages about 4 million Btu per capita per year,[65] but most of this energy is consumed by a small fraction of the urban population. Rural electrification programs are not extensive and mechanical irrigation is rare. Oil is the principal form of commercial energy, and with the major exceptions of Nigeria, Angola, and Gabon, most countries in tropical Africa must import their oil. Some, like Gambia, have not developed any indigenous source of commercial energy and must depend entirely on imported oil.

Oil-importing African countries have been among the hardest hit by the 1973–1974 increases in oil prices.[66] Some of them had hoped to obtain oil on concessional terms by severing relations with Israel during and after the October 1973 Arab-Israeli war. So far these hopes have not been fulfilled.

Kilombero, Tanzania*

The village of Kilombero on the Tanzanian plateau has 100 people who form 20 households. This small village, typical of Eastern Africa, has 60 hectares of non-irrigated land which is held in the form of a tribal trust. The chosen or traditional head of the village allocates the land to the household heads, and it may neither be mortgaged nor sold. The individual household heads have usufructary rights to the land which they forfeit if they leave it fallow for more than two years.

The people of Kilombero are far removed from any development efforts. The children under 14, who constitute half the population, contract diseases easily. Schistosomiasis, malaria, filariasis, respiratory tract infections, diarrhea, and overt malnutrition (usually in the form of kwashiorkor) are common causes of death.[67] Many of the common diseases are caused by a lack of clean domestic water supply. In this respect, and in many others, Kilombero is to be contrasted with the *Ujamaa* villages where the provision of sanitary water supply has been one of the principal improvements in the lives of the people. So far, however, only 15 to 20 percent of the rural population lives in *Ujamaa* villages, and life in Kilombero today is more representative of rural life in Tanzania and elsewhere in East Africa. The regular contacts with the people here have with the outside world are mostly those with the itinerant grain traders.

The population of Kilombero is growing at about 2 percent per year. This is somewhat slower than the East African population growth rate of 2.5 percent because of the migration to the cities. However, the rate of migration to the cities is smaller in Tanzania because, according to Tanzanian officials, the *Ujamaa* program offers them substantial incentives to remain in the villages.

---

*The principal references used in compiling this profile of a Tanzanian village were *The Village Economic Surveys, A Geography of Africa,* and the *Britannica World Atlas.* These are numbered 68, 69, and 70 in the notes for this chapter.

Possibly the deep attachment of the people to their land makes the task of the Tanzanian government easier than it would be, say, in Latin America.

Geography. Kilombero is located about 900 meters above sea level. At such an altitude, a vegetation of grass-land with broad-leaved deciduous plants predominates. The surface configuration consists of a plateau and steep slopes as one approaches the coast. The summers are hot (with cool nights); the winters are cool but rarely below freezing.

Because of its location on the Tanzanian plateau, Kilombero has certain advantages when compared with many other East African villages. Northern Tanzania, Uganda, Kenya, Somalia, and Ethiopia have been experiencing the effects of a severe drought which Kilombero has so far escaped. Also as a result of the cooler climates, the evaporation rates are lower than those on the coast, thereby increasing the water available to plants.

Kilombero receives from 60 to 90 centimeters of rain a year, concentrated in the summer months. There is a very high degree of rainfall variability, and Prothero states that "It is not unusual for the highest annual total to be as much as four times the lowest recorded total."[71]

Farming Conditions and Practices. Kilombero has no irrigation schemes. There is one well in the village which is used for domestic water. The two nearby streams, which are used to water the animals, dry up in the winter months. In times of prolonged drought (over two years of less than 50 percent of the average precipitation), villagers have to make a six-mile trek to a river for their water needs.

Kilombero villagers own 25 cattle. This is 40 percent fewer than the East African average, because the Tanzanian plateau is infested with the tsetse fly. The total livestock population of the village is shown in Table 2–10. Unlike the Hausa in Nigeria or the Chinese, the people of Kilombero do not make use of the animal wastes for fertilizing their fields. Animal droppings are not collected.

The people revere their cattle and regard them as a source of wealth. They are slaughtered only on special occasions. More frequently, they are bled, although blood is not as important a part of the diet here as it is with the Masai cattle herders.

Table 2-10. Livestock Population of Kilombero

Animals	Total	No. per Person
Cattle	20	.2
Poultry[a]	300	3
Goats	30	.3

[a]Chickens and ducks.

The tools used by the people in Kilombero includes hoes, axes, and bush knives known as *pangas*. The proportionate numbers of these tools used are shown in Table 2–11.

Energy. The energy put into the fields in Kilombero is among the lowest in the world, since only human labor is used. The total annual useful energy in agriculture, that is, the energy output of half the population at 170,000 Btu per person per year, would yield only 0.14 million Btu per hectare. In terms of the food eaten by the workers, however, the energy required is about 2.5 million Btu per hectare. This works out to about 3.5 million Btu per ton of maize which is one of the main crops grown in Kilombero.* This is comparable to the 3 million Btu/ton for corn grown in the U.S.A. (excluding crop processing and transportation).[72]

There is no electricity in Kilombero, and all fuel needs are satisfied through the use of firewood. Charcoal is not used. The woodfuel consumption runs to a total for Kilombero of about 150 tons a year, or about 1.5 tons per capita per year. Table 2–12 shows a summary of energy use in Kilombero.

Agricultural Production. The primary crops of the village of Kilombero are millet, maize, cassava, and peas. Crop yields are low (Table 2–13), and most of the output of the major crops of the village is locally consumed. Of the food production 20 percent or more is probably lost to pests due to inadequate storage and another 20 percent or so is sold to iternerant grain merchants in exchange for cash. On the basis of the average food production statistics, it appears that the caloric intake of the people of Kilombero is adequate and even the protein intake may approach adequacy in terms of weight, but not in terms of quality and completeness. However, average production statistics are misleading when we remember that the yields fluctuate widely from year to year and that in a year of drought food production could be cut in half.

Batagawara, Nigeria**

Batagawara is located in the Hausa region of Northern Nigeria and Southern Niger. This region is quite homogeneous, and conditions of one village are representative of other villages. It is perhaps the single largest homogenous region in tropical Africa, having existed under its present social order for many centuries. Its homogeneity in cultural, linguistic, and religious matters also

---

*Since one of the reasons for having many children is to provide a source of labor, we could justifiably include the food intake of all people to calculate the energy intensity. In that case the annual energy expended per hectare would be 7 million Btu and the energy per ton of maize about 10 million Btu.
**The principal reference for this village profile is Polly Hill's book *Rural Hausa: A Village and a Setting* (note 73).

Table 2-11.   Tools in the Village of Kilombero

Tool	Total	No. per Household
Hoes	60	3
Axes	15	.75
Pangas (bushknives)	30	1.5

Table 2-12.   Energy Use in Kilombero (Energy Use in Billion (10^9) Btu Except Row 13)

Energy Source	Useful Energy	Efficiency Percentage	Gross Energy Input
1. Animal labor	–	–	–
2. Woodfuel	0.11	5	2.2
3. Crop residues ⎱ direct use as fuel	–	–	–
4. Dung ⎰	–	–	–
5. Subtotal: noncommercial	0.11	5	2.2
6. Coal, oil, natural gas (direct use)	–	–	–
7. Electricity	–	–	–
8. Subtotal: commercial	–	–	–
9. Total: 5 + 8	0.11	5	2.2
10. Human energy	.008	2.5	0.3
11. Chemical fertilizers	–	–	–
12. Total energy use: 9 + 10 + 11	0.12	5	2.5
13. Per capita energy use per year.	1.2 million Btu	5	25 million Btu

Notes:
1. See Table 2-4.
2. We assume that 75 percent of the useful human energy is for farm work since agriculture is unassisted by animals or machines.

Table 2-13. Annual Food Production in Kilombero

Crop	Area Ha.	Yield Kg/ha.	Total Production Kg.
Maize	25	700	17,500
Millet	20	700	14,000
Cassava (wet)	3	6,000	18,000
Peas (dry)	2	300	600
Sunflower seeds	5	300	1,500
Beans (dry)	5	500	2,500

extends to the economic realm. Agricultural activity, for instance, is much the same throughout the Hausa region and has changed little over the years.

Batagawara, in the Emirate of Katsina, is about 20 miles south of the Niger border. The village has a total population of 1,400, of which 88 percent live in the village proper (*gari*) and the remaining 12 percent in dispersed housing in the farmland.

Almost half the population consists of children under 14 years of age. There are 170 households, and most of them have between 4 and 10 members. The 170 households of the village cultivate 530 hectares of manured land distributed among 530 plots. Land is privately held.

The subdivision of plots serves the social function of dividing up the good as well as the bad land among various owners. Batagawara villagers are well aware of the benefits of each farming unit comprising one continuous plot. In times of hardship when poor farmers have to sell their plots, wealthy farmers attempt to increase the size of their plot by buying or exchanging land to obtain plots adjacent to their own.

Batagawara has a rigid class-structure that is determined by the size and quality of the plot that the individual farmer controls. An advantage in land ownership generates other advantages in ownership of and access to other goods as exemplified by the ownership of plow-oxen and steel plows. Of the 170 households, 13 own and operate the 15 metal plows in the village. This particular situation exists with almost all mobile capital goods in the village. Thus, averages in production, acreage, or ownership of livestock are not representative of the lot of the average person. Inequitable distribution of land and wealth probably existed under the ancient system of land tenure in which land was regarded as the property of the community or clan (extended family). The introduction of private land ownership in colonial times, which has been continued in independent Nigeria, may have resulted in further inequities in income distribution.

Nigeria is, of course, the wealthiest major oil-producing country in tropical Africa, exporting most of the 2 million barrels a day it produces.[74] In 1974 Nigeria will earn in foreign exchange, roughly $5 billion for the export of this oil—or almost $100 per person per year. If Nigeria decides to give priority to agricultural development on which 65 percent of her people are directly dependent, it would be among the few underdeveloped nations to have enough capital to do the job within the next decade.

Geography.   Batagawara is located in a *semiarid tropical* region of West Africa. All months of the year are hot or warm, and there is light precipitation and rapid evaporation. It is a region of irregular plains and gentle slopes, generally less than 100 meters above sea level, where grass-land is the predominant vegetation.

Batagawara is near the southern border of the West African Sahel region that has suffered a devastating seven-year drought. The drought has not yet hit as hard here as it has to the North in Niger, Mali, Senegal, Upper Volta, Mauritania, and Chad. In 1974 the rains were better, but there is still considerable controversy over whether a long-term change in the climate of the region is taking place. Long-term reductions in rainfall along with a continuation of past neglect of the ecological realities of the spreading desert can only spell disaster for the people of this region. Batagawara, which is totally dependent on rain water for the nourishment of its crops, now receives about 50 centimeters of rain a year. Precipitation is concentrated in the late spring and summer months. There is as much as a two-month variation in the advent of the rains which may start as late as July or as early as May, ending sometime in September or October.

Farming Conditions and Practices. Fertilization is the backbone of Hausa agriculture. It is the reason why the Hausa have been able to continue to practice semi-intensive cultivation in the same region for several centuries without appreciable soil deterioration. Every scrap of material which is of manurial value is carefully preserved for use. The villagers own 100 cattle. In addition, every year the Fulani herdsmen of the surrounding region bring in about 400-500 cattle to graze in fallow Batagawara lands, for this they are paid a fee because the droppings of the cattle are left in the land where they graze. The herdsmen stay with their cattle in Batagawara for about seven months of the year. Chemical fertilizers, which were introduced here in the sixties, do not yet play a significant role in Hausa agriculture. Nigeria imports all the chemical fertilizers it uses, and their use has risen rapidly. But the use of chemical nitrogen fertilizers, for example, still averages less than one kilogram per hectare of cultivated land.[75]

Batagawara has no irrigation system. The wells in the village are used solely for domestic water supply. There is a total of six wells and four ponds in the village proper and the surrounding farmland. The water table is less than 20 meters from the ground surface.

Batagawara has no mechanically powered equipment. Field equipment consists of hand tools and equipment for the use of animal power. Livestock statistics for Batagawara are shown in Table 2–14.

There are about 0.35 hectares of manured farm-land per person. There is plenty of bushland surrounding the village that could be cleared for cultivation, but it would be unproductive without manure or chemical fertilizers. Most farmers therefore concentrate their efforts on the manured plots. However, some rice is cultivated in the marshland near the village. The production of rice is largely the work and responsibility of the women.

Energy. Most agricultural work is manual. As noted, the 36 plough oxen are owned by a few families, and the labor of these cattle is generally not available to most households. Energy flows on the farm are therefore similar to those we have already described for Kilombero, Tanzania.

Most of the fuel needs are satisfied through the use of fuel wood. Fuelwood consumption is about one metric ton per capita (15 million Btu). This is somewhat lower than Tanzanian fuel wood use and is probably due to the warmer climate. The wealthier people here have kerosene lamps and some have kerosene cooking stoves. Kerosene, like other urban goods, is purchased with the

Table 2–14. Livestock in Batagawara, Nigeria

Animals	Average No. per Household	Total for Village
Cattle	0.6	100
Plough oxen[a]	0.2	36^2
Pigs	0.3	50
Sheep	2.3	400
Goats	3.0	500

[a]Only the wealthiest of farmers own plough oxen, and most of the 36 plough oxen are owned by five or six households.

Table 2–15.   Energy Use in Batagawara, Nigeria (Energy Use in 10^9 Btu per Year Except Row 13)

Energy Source	Useful Energy	Efficiency Percentage	Gross Energy Input
1. Animal labor	0.05	5	1
2. Woodfuel	1.05	5	21
3. Crop residues } direct use as fuel	–	–	–
4. Dung	–	–	–
5. Subtotal: noncommercial	1.1	5	22
6. Kerosene (primarily cooking and some lighting)	0.01	20	0.05
7. Electricity	–	–	–
8. Subtotal: commercial	0.01	20	0.05
9. Total: 5 + 8	1.1	5	22
10. Human energy	0.1	2.5	4
11. Chemical fertilizers	0.1	–	0.1
12. Total energy use: 9 + 10 + 11	1.3	5	26.1
13. Per capita energy use per year	0.9 million Btu	5	18.5 million Btu

Notes:

1. We assume that the per capita use of wood in Batagawara is 15 million Btu per year, i.e., the same as that in the Gambia in Western Africa.

2. We assume that 75 percent of the human energy (useful) is for farm work since most farm work is unassisted by animals or mechanically powered equipment.

Table 2-16.   Agricultural Production in Batagawara

Crop	Hectares	Annual Yield kg/ha	Annual Production m.t.	Annual per capita Production kg.
Millet	200	600	120	85
Maize	200	1,000	200	140
Groundnuts in shell	120	700	84	60
Vegetables and fruits	10	variable	small	small
Rice	10	~1,000?	10?	7?

proceeds ortained from the sale of groundnuts. A summary of energy use in Batagawara is shown in Table 2–15.

Agricultural Production. The main crops of Batagawara village are millet, maize, and groundnuts. There is some production of rice, fruits, and assorted vegetables, but the bulk of the farmland is dedicated to the first three. The yields of groundnuts have declined substantially since the early sixties. With the exception of groundnuts, most of the produce is internally consumed. Production statistics are shown in Table 2–16.

Because of the groundnuts consumed here, the diet of the people, in good years, is probably of a higher quality than that available to the people of Kilombero, Tanzania.

LATIN AMERICA

Agriculture is the main source of livelihood for 40 to 50 percent of Latin America's population of 300 million.[76] The population of Latin America is growing at about 3 percent per year, more rapidly than any other major region of the world. The cities bear the brunt of this population growth, and rural migration has caused the creation of widespread shanty towns, or *villas miserias,* as they are often called. Approximately 5 million families live in these *villas miserias;* and this portion of the population is growing at about 15 percent per year.

In spite of this migration to the cities, the rural population has been growing at 1.5 percent per year. This population growth rate would not by itself cause serious land problems since the cultivated area is about 0.6 hectares per capita (of rural population) and the potential for its expansion is large in many areas.[77] It is the inequitable distribution of land holdings and capital that is mainly responsible for rural poverty. A recent study[78] revealed that in seven Latin American countries 21 percent of the farm units controlled 56.4 percent of the cultivated land, while 60.3 percent of the farm units contained only 6.6

percent of the area. The private large farms (*latifundia*) have been dismantled in Cuba and to some extent in Bolivia, Mexico, Peru, and Chile, but they are still common in most Latin American countries. Without land reform and a redirection of capital toward the smaller farmer, we cannot expect much alleviation of the poverty, particularly in Latin America where the small farms (*minifundia*) are scattered over the countryside amidst the *latifundia*. This pattern of land settlement puts a premium on land reform and political reorganization, because without them capital investments on the farms, roads, communications, irrigation, or rural electrification will be more expensive and less productive, even if the additional capital were to become available to the small farmer. This is perhaps most valid in many Latin American countries where, on the one hand, owners of the *latifundia* who live in the cities are reluctant to invest in the countryside, and on the other hand, the small farms are scattered all over the countryside making improvements such as roads or electrification more expensive than they would be in larger settlements.

It is important to note that land distribution influences the differences in land productivity *within a region*. The differences between regions and countries, as we shall see, are much more dependent on whether development policies favor the provision of inputs such as irrigation, fuel, and fertilizers to the countryside. In other words, if the capital is not directed towards agricultural development and if it is not spent in a manner that is consonant with the potential of the region, agricultural development will be slow and the majority of the rural population will remain poor.

Farming conditions in Latin America are perhaps more varied than elsewhere in the Third World. We have dramatized these differences by studying a village (*ejido*) in Mexico that has irrigation, fertilizers, commercial fuels, and high-yielding seeds available, and a *minifundio* in Bolivia where the people are as poor as most small farmers in South Asia and Africa.

However, the differences in rural income in Northern Mexico on the one hand, and Southern Mexico and Bolivia on the other, cannot be due solely to inequitable land distribution because substantial land reforms have taken place in these areas. In fact, the land holdings are considerably more concentrated in Northern Mexico where the larger landowners have gradually bought out the small farmers, a trend which has accelerated since the introduction of the high yielding grain varieties.[79] The differences between these regions can be directly attributed to government policies toward agricultural development. In Northern Mexico, continual efforts at irrigation, provision of fertilizers, high yielding seeds, and so on, have made a naturally arid soil productive. South of Mexico City and in Bolivia where the rainfall is more abundant, the soil richer and the land holdings better distributed, the people are much poorer. Most farms do not have irrigation or electricity or farm machinery.

Information on the use of noncommercial energy sources in Latin America is scarce. We know of no surveys that have been conducted. However, it appears that wood and other vegetable matter are the main fuels for most of Latin America's rural population. In the Andes, wide use is made of the scrub plants that grow above the treeline. Where the climate is cold (Andean region, the regions of high altitude in Central America, and South of 20°S latitude generally) we can infer from the Tanzanian data that the use of wood (or plants) is likely to be considerably more than one metric ton per capita. We will assume that in these regions, the use of wood and shrubs for cooking and heating is about 25 million Btu per year per person.

The use of commercial energy is 22 million Btu per capita in Latin American compared to 6 million Btu/capita in South Asia and 4 million Btu/capita in Africa.[80] But the average numbers are misleading because a disproportionately large amount of commercial energy is used by the relatively well-to-do. Electricity use, for example, is about 650 kwhe/yr/capita in Latin America, yet only about 2 percent of the total electricity generated is consumed in the rural areas where 40 to 50 percent of the people live.[81] Thus the availability of electricity to the farmer and his use of it in Latin America is about the same as in India, where 10 percent of the electricity is used in the countryside, but the total per capita generation is only one-sixth that of Latin America. This is yet another symptom of the maldistribution of income that is endemic in much of the Third World, and which is particularly egregious in many parts of Latin America such as Brazil (Chapter One).

Arango, Mexico

Northern Mexico, where Arango is located, is the birthplace of the Green Revolution for tropical countries. Arango was established in 1934 as a collective *ejido* (village), but the land is now held or leased by individual *ejidatarios* (heads of household). The *ejidos* as collectives withered away in the forties and fifties due to antipathy on the part of the central government, mismanagement, lack of effective extension services, the peasant's desire to have his own piece of land, and the preferential lending policies of the Ejido Bank to individual *ejidatarios*.[82]

The 80 *ejidatarios* of Arango (420 people) have 380 hectares of irrigated land, and the average holding is 4.8 hectares. The smallest farm is 4 hectares and the largest is 7 hectares—a spread which is remarkably small compared to other parts of Latin America and the Third World in general. Arango also has 700 hectares of unirrigated land.

Arango is a rich community by the standards of most of the rural population of the Third World. We analyze it here to illustrate the dramatic differences that high-yielding seeds (particularly wheat), irrigation water, fertilizers, and fuel have made to the lives of millions of farmers in Mexico and elsewhere, in spite of the maldistribution of the resultant wealth and many other individual and institutional inequities that, in Mexico, persist 20 years after the initiation of the Green Revolution.

The conditions on the *minifundio* (small farm), which is perhaps more representative of the lot of the Latin American peasant, are considerably more unpleasant (next case study).

Geography.   The Laguna region has an arid subtropical climate with hot summers and relatively cool winters. The annual rainfall is only about 30 centimeters. Unirrigated land produces a meager harvest due to the scanty rainfall and is therefore not cultivated, particularly as surpluses of wheat are produced by the use of high-yielding varieties on the irrigated land.

The soil of Arango is typical of over 50 percent of Mexico: "desertic soil, of arid climate, which includes many areas of shallow stony soil. There is sparce cover of shrubs and grass, some suitable for grazing; it is fertile if irrigated; dry farming is possible in some areas."[83]

Farming Conditions and Practices.   Most of Arango's cultivated land is irrigated by an intricate system of canals fed by the Nazas river, which never runs dry; 30 percent is irrigated from the six wells in the *ejido,* and the remaining 10 percent from the Aguanaval River which is dry in December and January. Irrigation has freed the *ejidatarios* from the vagaries of the highly variable and scant rainfall in the region and enabled them to use high-yielding seed varities and fertilizers in a farming cycle that is largely under human control. However, the level of the water table in the region is dropping, and there is the danger that it may be of little use in the foreseeable future.[84] Wilkie classifies much of the Arango's underground water supply as unusable for irrigation[85] but does not cite precise information on this score so that we cannot judge whether future expansion of the irrigation water supply is possible with improved technical inputs.

Farm machinery is widely employed, as are fertilizers and pesticides. Draft animals (Table 2–17) mingle with machines in providing labor for farms, but most of the 400 horsepower for the farms comes from machines. In addition there are mechanical irrigation pumps with a total of about 100 horsepower. We

Table 2-17.   Livestock Population in Arango

Livestock	Total in ejido
Mules, burros, horses	80
Oxen	30
Dairy cattle	20
Hogs	20
Poultry	350

Note: The cattle in Arango are primarily draft animals, and their number is considerably lower than a national average would indicate because most cattle in Mexico are beef and milk cattle.

have found no evidence to indicate that animal dung is used either for its fertilizer or fuel potential.

Energy. As with fertilizers and irrigation water, so with fuels: the people of Arango use substantially more commercial energy than their counterparts in most Third World villages. Each home has a kerosene lamp, half have (potable) running water, one-fifth have electricity, and one-third have gas stoves. Many families spend $50 or more a year on gas, kerosene, and electricity. Two-thirds of the people still heat their houses and cook by burning agricultural wastes such as cotton stubble. The fires are usually lighted in the doorway. Two or three decades ago it was common for Indian farm laborers to collect wood in the forests during the off-season (winter) and bring it on mule-back to the *ejido,* but we could not determine whether this is still common practice in the Laguna region.

The largest *indirect* energy input *imported into* the *ejido* comes in the form of chemical fertilizer. One hundred twenty kg/ha. are commonly used for the high-yielding wheat varieties which are in almost universal use in this region.

Table 2–18 shows a summary of energy use in Arango. We note that while the consumption of commercial and noncommercial energy in Arango is similar, the commercial energy provides 80 percent of the useful energy.

Agricultural Production. The principal crops of the *ejido* are corn, cotton, beans, and winter wheat (Table 2–19). Other crops are grown in small quantities. In the summer growing season (June through September), half the acreage is devoted to cotton, 30 percent to corn, 8 percent to beans, and 12 percent to miscellaneous other crops. In the winter (November through April), about 50 percent of the land is planted with winter wheat, and the remaining 50 percent is apparently left fallow. It is not clear whether this is done because of the lack of sufficient water during those months to irrigate more than 50 percent of the land or because farmers want to give part of the land a rest.

Most of the agricultural production is exported to the cities either through private traders or the Ejido Bank. It is this considerable surplus production that is responsible for the relative prosperity of farmers in the Laguna region of Northern Mexico. In fact, most of the food for Mexican cities and towns in provided by surpluses of relatively few farmers who, by and large, live in Northern Mexico.

Quebrada, Bolivia

Unlike all our previous prototypical villages, where we dealt with communities, this example is about an isolated household, or *minifundio,* not physically part of a community. In Bolivia, *minifundios* resulted from the fragmentation of land that followed the Agrarian Reform of 1952. *Minifundios* also developed as a result of the acquisition of land by large landowners that pushed

Table 2-18. Energy Use in Arango, Mexico (Energy Use in 10^9 Btu per Year Except Row 13)

Energy Source	Useful Energy	Efficiency Percentage	Gross Energy Input
1. Animal labor	0.15	5	3
2. Woodfuel and crop residues[a]	0.3	5	6
3. Subtotal: noncommercial	0.45	5	9
4. Oil for farm machines[b]	0.6	20	3
5. Kerosene for lighting[c]	small	small ($\leqslant$1)	0.3
6. Electricity for irrigation	1.6	20	8
7. Household electricity[d]	0.03	20	0.15
8. Household gas (primarily for heating)[e]	0.35	50	0.7
9. Subtotal: commercial	2.6	22	12.15
10. Human energy[f]	0.05	3	1.5
11. Chemical fertilizers[g]	3.3	—	3.3
12. Total: 3 + 9 + 10 + 11	6.4	25	25.95
13. Per capita energy use per year	15.2 million Btu	25	62 million Btu

Note: At $1/million Btu for gas and 2¢/kwhe for electricity, a household having both would spend about $75 per year on gas and electricity.

[a]We assume that two-thirds of the people who cook and heat their homes with wood crop residues use about 20 million Btu/capita/yr.

[b]The total land involved is about 550 ha. (including double cropping), of which roughly 100 ha. is worked by draft animals.

[c]3 million Btu/household per year, assuming one lamp operating five hours/day.

[d]For the households that have electricity (20 percent) we use an average of 500 kwhe/hr for domestic electricity use (assuming that 20 percent of the electricity use in Mexico is for domestic purposes).

[e]We assume that the households that have gas use it both for heating and cooking. We assume average gas use is 5 million Btu/capita per year, of which cooking uses 20 percent. At a heating efficiency of 50 percent the useful heat would thus be about 10 million Btu/yr/household compared to less than half that for homes heated with wood.

[f]At 10,000 Btu (2,500 kcal) per person per day.

[g]One hundred twenty kg/ha of nitrogen for wheat; 50 kg/ha for corn and cotton yields a total nitrogen fertilizer use of about 40 metric tons. Phosphorous and potassium together also amount to about 40 tons.

See also notes to Tables 2-4 and 2-8.

Table 2-19. Output of Major Crops in Arango

Crop	Yield kg/ha.	Area: ha.	Annual Production Metric Tons
Cotton	500	190	95
Beans (dry)	600	30	18
Winter wheat	3,000	220	660
Maize	2,500	110	275

many peasants to progressively smaller holdings—a situation compounded by population growth and the resultant subdivision.

The Quebrada (canyon) region lies between the High Plateau of the Andes and the flatlands of Ilanos. The Quebradas are populated by peasants of indigenous American stock, and the region is over 90 percent rural. Few urban centers exist, and those that do exist are primarily market towns.

Although the range of *minifundio* sizes is large, 1 hectare of cultivated land is representative, and we use this for our analysis. The *parcela* (the household and the land attached to it) we study has six people.

Geography. Quebrada lies between the altitudes of 1,000 and 2,500 meters in a mountaneous region of sharp relief. It has a mild temperate climate and an annual precipitation of 85 to 110 centimeters which is concentrated in the summer (December-February). The rivers and streams become torrents during the rainy season and generally have some flow throughout the year.

Farming Conditions and Practices. The many streams and rivers of the region are exploited for irrigation. Gravity irrigation, with dikes diverting water into canals and irrigation ditches, is one of the principal methods, so that the energy for water irrigation is largely provided for by nature. Dikes have to be rebuilt frequently, particularly after heavy rains.[86] However, irrigation is not widespread in Bolivia. In 1950, the latest year for which we have data, only 5 percent of the cultivated land was irrigated.[87]

Chemical fertilizers are not common. We could not determine whether animal dung is collected either for fuel or fertilizer.

Livestock are precious, not only as an investment but as a source of food, lard, tallow, wool, hides, feathers (Table 2–20). Some peasants grow alfalfa, but the livestock feeds mostly on the scattered and poor quality grass of the region which grows scarcer with increasing altitude.

Farms are not mechanized. Farm implements are limited to shovels, picks, hoes, and plows, which are usually wooden and made in the small towns of the region.

Energy. Unlike Arango, farm animals are the main source of farm labor in Quebrada. In this sense, as well as in the subsistence nature of the *minifundio* economy, the life of the people here is much like that of peasants in South Asia. The farm animals provide not only the field work but also the

Table 2-20. Livestock on a *Parcela*

Dairy cattle	1
Draft animals (horses, mules, donkeys)	3
Sheep	3
Pigs	2
Rabbits	5
Poultry	7

transportation. Since Quebrada is a mountainous region and since the *mini-fundios* are usually quite far from the market towns, we would guess that a substantial portion of the energy output of the draft animals is devoted to transportation.

Wood is the primary source of heat, and in the higher altitudes *tola* is used, a sturdy bush that has low moisture content. Fires are harder to start and to keep going at higher altitudes; cooking also requires greater use of fuel, since foodstuffs must be cooked longer. The use of firewood is probably over two tons per year per capita since the winters are cold. (In nineteenth century United States, when firewood was the main source of fuel, the yearly use of firewood per person was about three tons, most of which was probably used for domestic heating and cooking).[88]

Peasants fight the cold weather mostly by using heavy woolen sweaters made of the warm alpaca and llama wool. A summary of energy use on a parcela is shown in Table 2–21.

Agricultural Production. Maize, potatoes, wheat, and barley are the main crops accounting for 75 percent of the cultivated land; the remaining 25 percent is divided between manioc (cassava), vegetables, and fruit trees. Some of

Table 2-21. Energy Use on a *Parcela* in Quebrada, Bolivia

Energy Source	Useful Energy	Efficiency Percentage	Gross Energy Input
1. Animal labor (including transportation)[a,b]	3	5	60
2. Woodfuel	10	5	200
3. Crop residues ⎫ direct use as fuel ⎱	–	–	–
4. Dung ⎭	–	–	–
5. Subtotal: noncommercial	13	5	260
6. Coal, oil, natural gas (direct use)	–	–	–
7. Electricity	–	–	–
8. Subtotal: commercial	–	–	–
9. Total: 5 + 8	13	5	260
10. Human energy	0.5	2.5	20
11. Chemical fertilizers	–	–	–
12. Total energy use: 9 + 10 + 11	13.5	5	280
13. Per capita energy use	2.3	5	47

Notes: See Table 2–4.

[a]We assume that 50 percent of the animal labor (useful) and 50 percent of the human labor (useful) is for farm activities.

[b]Since mules and donkeys are somewhat smaller animals than horses and draft cattle, we assume an annual energy intake of 20 million Btu/mule or donkey.

Table 2-22. Agricultural Production on a One-Hectare *Parcela*

Crop	Amount of Land Hectares	Yield kg/ha.	Annual Production kg.	Gross Annual Production per Capita kg.
Maize	0.25	1,000	250	42
Potatoes	0.25	4,000	1,000	170
Wheat	0.1	700	70	12
Groundnuts (in shell)	0.05	1,500	75	12
Dry beans	0.1	700	70	12
Grapes	0.05	6,000	300	60
Cassava (wet)	0.2	10,000	2,000	330

the produce is sold in the towns, and a few products, such as grapes, form the bases of growing market town industries.

The amount of land allocated to each crop varies with the altitude; potatoes replace fruits and some vegetables at higher altitudes.

Table 2–22 shows the agricultural production on a parcela with fair farming conditions and partial irrigation. Though the *minifundio* has some surplus to sell, present circumstances make increasing this surplus expensive, and a transition to an economy similar to the Mexican *ejido* seems difficult or impossible without larger settlements, investments in agriculture, and the development of market towns.

ANALYSIS OF VILLAGE ENERGY USE

The village case studies show that most of the energy used in rural areas is for domestic cooking and heating. Wood and other vegetable matter, crop residues, and (in North India) cattle dung are the main sources of domestic fuel. From an engineering standpoint this energy is used inefficiently and the yield of useful energy, which is the desired commodity, is small. We reemphasize that inefficiency is used here in a technical sense only. The energy is essential to the villager for the maintenance of life today and he usually has neither the capital nor technical knowledge to obtain a higher yield of useful energy. From the economic standpoint of the individual, therefore, the villager may be making the best use of the available resources, even though such use by millions of people is often seriously detrimental to the land in the long run. This is the problem of the commons, where each person must use a common pasture to survive, resulting in the death of an overgrazed pasture. It is a problem similar to the one that results in the pollution of air and water resources, but it appears in a much more urgent and immediate form every day to the villager of the Third World. Many problems of development policy resemble the commons problem and reflect the universal necessity of people in poverty to attend to today's problems, for their very existence would be in jeopardy if they did not.

For the two countries for which the data are available (India and Gambia), the use of noncommercial energy for cooking is quite similar—5 to 7 million Btu per capita per year. It would appear, therefore, that the main variations in noncommercial energy use arise from differences in climate, more fuel being required for heating in colder climates. In areas where fuel is in short supply, fuel use for heating is low even though the climate may be quite cold. Per capita energy use variations linked with variations in climate are not directly related to the productivity of the land. In fact, other things being equal, warmer climates have the potential of producing considerably more thorough multiple cropping.

Next to climate, the most important factor in rural energy use is the energy used in agriculture. This depends as much on the amount of land cultivated as on the technology of cultivation. The lowest energy input per hectare is associated with agriculture unassisted by animal labor or farm machines. The use of animals to supplement human labor, of course, increases energy use per unit of land, but tractors, *when used as a substitute for animal labor,* decrease the energy requirements.*

Tables 2–23, 2–24, and 2–25 compare the energy use in the production of rice, wheat, and maize in the six prototypical villages.

In order to eliminate some sources of error, we compare production only if a significant portion of the land and labor is devoted to that crop. Crop processing (threshing, drying, etc.) and transportation energy requirements are not included because we wish to examine the effect of energy input to farms on land productivity. These tables, which are based on the data presented earlier in this chapter, show the gross energy inputs per hectare for farm work, irrigation, and fertilizers (organic and chemical), the gross energy input per ton of produce, and the useful energy per ton and per hectare of land.**

Tropical Africa has the smallest input of energy (both gross and useful) into farm work. The gross energy requirements increase with the use of draft animals and decrease where tractors are used in place of draft animals. The useful energy input to farm work does not vary much between the places where animals and tractors are used. This is probably more dependent on soil conditions and topography, as long as there is some source of energy to supplement human labor.

The differences in land productivity appear to be largely connected with the mix of energy inputs to the farm and the efficiency of the use of the

*This does not make any statement about the energy source used to run the tractor. Crop residues can be substituted for petroleum and the effect on energy requirements will be similar.
**Note that for fertilizers and irrigation we have used the energy accounting procedure discussed in Appendix A and summarized in the notes to Table 2–23. In particular see note 4, Table 2–23.

Table 2-23. Comparative Analysis of Energy Use in Rice Production

Place	Gross per Capita Energy Use 10^6 Btu/yr.	Yield kg/ha	Gross Energy Input to Farms 10^6 Btu/ha				Gross Energy Input to Farms 10^6 Btu/ton	Total Useful Energy Input to Farms	
			Farm Work	Irrigation	Fertilizer	Total		10^6 Btu/ton	10^6 Btu/ha
Mangaon, India	14.7	850	21.2 (including irrigation)		0.5	21.7	25.6	1.7	1.4
Peipan, China	31.5	3,000	17.5	15	8	40.5	13.5	4	12.1

Notes:

1. This table is derived from the data shown on the village case studies. As noted in the beginning of Chapter Two, the data are indicative rather than definitive.

2. The energy use on farms has been allocated equally among the various crops. Since we are considering only the crops to which major fractions of the cultivated land are devoted, this approximation should not result in major errors.

3. We have assumed that the energy input for mechanized irrigation is 15 million Btu/crop/ha. The corresponding useful energy is 3 million Btu.

4. The energy requirements for nitrogen fertilizers are 75 million Btu/ton of nitrogen. We have added 10 percent to this to take into account (approximately) the energy requirements for phosphorous and potassium. *In order that organic and chemical fertilizers be shown on an equivalent basis, we have used the same numbers per unit of fertilizers whether they have chemical or organic sources.* This is a major difference between Tables 2-23, 2-24, 2-25, and 2-26 on the one hand, and Tables 2-4, 2-8, 2-12, 2-15, 2-18, and 2-22 on the other. In the latter tables we have shown the energy required to manufacture chemical fertilizers, but organic fertilizers do not appear in the calculations.

5. Any irrigation that is powered by human and animal labor is included in the category "farm work."

Table 2-24.   Comparative Analysis of Energy Use in Wheat Production

Place	Gross per Capita Energy Use 10⁶ Btu/yr.	Yield kg/ha	Gross Energy Input to Farms 10⁶ Btu/ha				Gross Energy Input to Farms 10⁶ Btu/ton	Total Useful Energy Input to Farms	
			Farm Work	Irrigation	Fertilizer	Total		10⁶ Btu/ton	10⁶ Btu/ha
Mangaon, India	14.7	850	21.2		0.5	21.7	25.6	1.7	1.4
Peipan, China	31.5	1,000	17.5	5	2	24.5	24.5	4.1	4.1
Arango, Mexico	62	3,000	10.2	15	10	35.2	11.7	3.8	14.3
Quebrada, Bolivia	47	700	35			35	50	2.5	1.8

Notes:

1. This table is derived from the data shown on the village case studies. As noted in the beginning of Chapter Two, the data are indicative rather than definitive.

2. The energy use on farms has been allocated equally among the various crops. Since we are considering only the crops to which major fractions of the cultivated land are devoted, this approximation should not result in major errors.

3. We have assumed that the energy input for mechanized irrigation is 15 million Btu/crop/ha. The corresponding useful energy is 3 million Btu.

4. The energy requirements for nitrogen fertilizers are 75 million Btu/ton of nitrogen. We have added 10 percent to this to take into account (approximately) the energy requirements for phosphorous and potassium. *In order that organic and chemical fertilizers be shown on an equivalent basis, we have used the same numbers per unit of fertilizers whether they have chemical or organic sources.* This is a major difference between Tables 2–23, 2–24, 2–25, and 2–26 on the one hand, and Tables 2–4, 2–8, 2–12, 2–15, 2–18, and 2–22 on the other. In the latter tables we have shown the energy required to manufacture chemical fertilizers, but organic fertilizers do not appear in the calculations.

5. Any irrigation that is powered by human and animal labor is included in the category "farm work."

Table 2-25. Comparative Analysis of Energy Use in Maize Production

Place	Gross per Capita Energy Use 10^6 Btu/yr.	Yield kg/ha	Gross Energy Input to Farms 10^6 Btu/ha				Gross Energy Input to Farms 10^6 Btu/ton	Total Useful Energy Input to Farms	
			Farm Work	Irrigation	Fertilizer	Total		10^6 Btu/ton	10^6 Btu/ha
Mangaon, India	14.7	1,100	21.2		0.5	21.7	19.9	1.3	1.4
Peipan, China	31.5	2,500	17.5	10	4	31.5	12.6	2.4	6.1
Kilombero, Tanzania	25	700	3.8	0		3.8	5.5	0.14	0.1
Batagawara, Nigeria	18.5	1,000	4.7	0	4.5	9.2	9.2	4.7	4.7
Arango, Mexico	62	2,500	10.2	15	4.5	29.7	11.9	3.5	8.8
Quebrada, Bolivia	47	1,000	35			35	35	1.8	1.8

Notes:

1. This table is derived from the data shown on the village case studies. As noted in the beginning of Chapter Two, the data are indicative rather than definitive.

2. The energy use on farms has been allocated equally among the various crops. Since we are considering only the crops to which major fractions of the cultivated land are devoted, this approximation should not result in major errors.

3. We have assumed that the energy input for mechanized irrigation is 15 million Btu/crop/ha. The corresponding useful energy is 3 million Btu.

4. The energy requirements for nitrogen fertilizers are 75 million Btu/ton of nitrogen. We have added 10 percent to this to take into account (approximately) the energy requirements for phosphorous and potassium. *In order that organic and chemical fertilizers be shown on an equivalent basis, we have used the same numbers per unit of fertilizers whether they have chemical or organic sources.* This is a major difference between Tables 2–23, 2–24, 2–25, and 2–26 on the one hand, and Tables 2–4, 2–8, 2–12, 2–15, 2–18, and 2–22 on the other. In the latter tables we have shown the energy required to manufacture chemical fertilizers, but organic fertilizers do not appear in the calculations.

5. Any irrigation that is powered by human and animal labor is included in the category "farm work."

energy input. As anticipated, irrigation and fertilizers increase energy inputs (we have also counted organic fertilizer in energy equivalent terms), but the total energy requirements per ton of grain are lower—that is, the energy intensity decreases (Figure 2–2). Rather, land productivity appears to be related to useful energy inputs to the land (Figure 2–3). This, of course, is not to say that indiscriminate increases in fertilizers will decrease the energy intensity or increase the yields, but within the range shown and the limitations of the data, this seems a sound conclusion.

We have not explicitly included the effect of seed varieties in these calculations. To some extent differences in seed varieties are implicit, since it is the high-yielding varieties that usually respond well to applications of fertilizers and irrigation. But the seeds must suit local conditions and unless they are available or local varieties are significantly responsive to higher inputs of fertilizer, the useful energy inputs may be high, but the yields will not be correspondingly higher. High-yielding seed varieties are, in effect, a way in which plant genetics is used to trap solar energy more efficiently. Thus, in China where suitable varieties of wheat are not yet in widespread use,[89] wheat yields are relatively low,[90] despite the irrigation and fertilizers. This is in contrast to Chinese rice and maize production or to wheat production in Northern Mexico.

The proper understanding and use of energy is only one essential aspect of a productive agriculture. Of course, proper management, capital, suitable seed varieties, pest control, etc., also make essential contributions to a

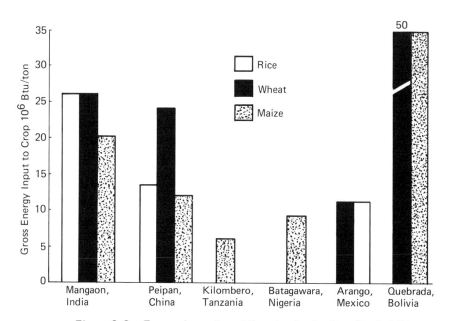

Figure 2-2. Energy Intensity of Farming in the Case Study Villages

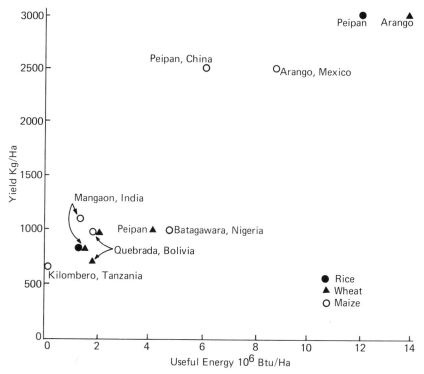

Figure 2-3. Yield and Useful Energy for Three Grains: Case Study Results

more efficient harnessing of solar energy in the form of food. The potential for so doing is great, for in the tropical countries where more than 300 frost-free days are the rule rather than the exception, many crops a year should be possible. Indeed, in some places such as Southern China, Taiwan, Northern Mexico, and Punjab, much of this potential is already being realized. In subsequent chapters we shall analyze energy needs for agricultural development, the sources of energy supply, and the implications for development policy.

Notes to Chapter Two

1. Stewart Odend'hal, "Energetics of Indian Cattle in Their Environment," *Human Ecology* 1 (1972).

2. Herman Southworth (ed.), *Farm Mechanization in East Asia* (New York: Agricultural Development Council, 1972).

3. F. B. Morrisson, *Feeds and Feeding* (Ithaca, N.Y.: Morrisson Publishing Co., 1947).

4. David Pimentel et al., "Food Production and the Energy Crisis," *Science* (2 November 1973).

5. *Production Yearbook 1972*, Vol. 26 (Rome: Food and Agriculture Organization of the United Nations, 1973).

6. Keith Openshaw, "The Gambia: A Wood Consumption Survey and Timber Trend Study 1973–2000," Unpublished report to the ODA/LRD Gambia Land Resources Development Project, Midlothian, Great Britain, 1973.

7. Keith Openshaw, "Projections of Wood Use in Tanzania," Unpublished report to the Public Works Department, Tanzania, Midlothian, Great Britain, 1973.

8. Keith Openshaw, "Projections of Wood Use in Thailand," Unpublished report to the Public Works Department, Thailand, Midlothian, Great Britain, 1973.

9. *Report of the Energy Survey of India Committee* (New Delhi: Government of India, 1965).

10. *World Energy Supplies 1960–1970,* Statistical Papers, Series J, No. 15 (New York: United Nations, 1971).

11. *Ibid.*

12. Lester Brown, *By Bread Alone* (Washington, D.C.: Overseas Development Council, 1974).

13. *India 1971–72* (New Delhi: Government of India, 1972).

14. Mohindar S. Mudahar, "Dynamic Analysis of Agricultural Revolution in Punjab, India," Cornell University, Ithaca, New York, July 1974.

15. *Ibid.*

16. *India 1971–72.*

17. K. L. Rao, "Irrigation" (New Delhi: Government of India, 1972).

18. Ranjit Gupta, *The Musahri Plan* (Patna, India: Association of Voluntary Agencies for Rural Development, 1972).

19. *India 1971–72.*

20. *Economic Situation and Prospects for India—Vol. II: The Energy Sector* (Washington, D.C.: International Bank for Reconstruction and Development, 1974).

21. S. Swayambu, "Power Development," (New Delhi: Government of India, 1972).

22. Planning Commission, *Report on Evaluation of the Rural Electrification Programme* (New Delhi: Government of India, 1965).

23. *Report of the Energy Survey.*

24. *World Energy Supplies 1960–1970.*

25. Gilbert Etienne, *Studies in Indian Agriculture* (Berkeley: University of California Press, 1968).

26. Gupta, *The Musahri Plan.*

27. Rao, "Irrigation."

28. Brown, *By Bread Alone.*

29. L. K. Sen et al., *Planning Rural Growth Centers for Integrated Area Development* (Hyderabad, India: National Institute for Community Development, 1971).

30. Gupta, *The Musahri Plan.*

31. Owen L. Dawson, *Communist China's Agriculture* (New York: Praeger, 1970).
32. Leslie Kuo, *The Technical Transformation of Communist China's Agriculture* (New York: Praeger, 1972).
33. Leo Goodstadt, *China's Search for Plenty* (New York: John Weatherhill, 1972).
34. Mao Tse-Tung, *Selected Works of Mao Tse-Tung*, Foreign Languages Press, Peking.
35. Goodstadt, *China's Search,* pp. 58–64.
36. Dawson, *Communist China's Agriculture.*
37. Goodstadt, *China's Search.*
38. F. H. King, *Farmers of Forty Centuries* (Emmaus, Pa: Rodale Press, 1911).
39. Goodstadt, *China's Search.*
40. *Ibid.*
41. King, *Farmers.*
42. Dawson, *Communist China's Agriculture.*
43. *World Energy Supplies 1960–1970.*
44. Dawson, *Communist China's Agriculture.*
45. Etienne, *Studies.*
46. Dawson, *Communist China's Agriculture,* pp. 312–314.
47. S. D. Richardson, *Forestry in Communist China* (Baltimore, Md.: Johns Hopkins Press, 1966).
48. *Ibid.,* p. 66.
49. *Ibid.,* pp. 168–169.
50. Dawson, *Communist China's Agriculture.*
51. Richardson, *Forestry.*
52. Dawson, *Communist China's Agriculture.*
53. *Production Yearbook 1972.*
54. Dawson, *Communist China's Agriculture.*
55. D. F. Owen, *Man in Tropical Africa* (New York: Oxford University Press, 1973).
56. *Ibid.*
57. *Ibid.,* p. 15.
58. Mwalimu Nyerere, *The Arusha Declaration* (Washington, D.C.: Embassy of Tanzania, n.d.).
59. Henry Bienen, *Tanzania* (Princeton, N.J.: Princeton University Press, 1970).
60. Roger Revelle et al. "Water and Land," Chapter 7 in *The World Food Problem,* Vol. II, U.S. Government Printing Office, Washington, D.C., 1967.
61. R. F. Dasmann, J. P. Milton, and P. H. Freeman, *Ecological Principles for Economic Development* (New York: John Wiley, 1973).
62. Owen, *Man in Tropical Africa,* p. 119.
63. *World Energy Supplies 1960–1970.*
64. Owen, *Man in Tropical Africa,* p. 37.
65. *World Energy Supplies 1960–1970.*
66. World Bank, "Additional Capital Requirements of Developing Countries," Washington, D. C., March 1974.

67. Owen, *Man in Tropical Africa.*
68. Tanganyika Central Statistical Bureau, *Village Economic Surveys, 1961–1962.*
69. R. M. Prothero, ed., *A Geography of Africa* (London: Routledge & Keagan Paul, 1973).
70. *Britannica World Atlas,* Encyclopedia Britannica, W. Benton, 1972.
71. Prothero, *A Geography,* p. 209.
72. Pimentel et al., "Food Production and the Energy Crisis."
73. Polly Hill, *Rural Hausa: A Village and a Setting* (London: Cambridge University Press, 1972).
74. "1973: The Year of Major Changes in Worldwide Oil," *Gas and Oil Journal* 71 (December 1973).
75. *Production Yearbook 1972.*
76. P. Dorner, *Land Reform and Economic Development* (New York: Penguin, 1972).
77. Revelle et al., "Water and Land."
78. Dorner, *Land Reform.*
79. Cynthia Hewitt, *The Social and Economic Implications of Large Scale Introduction of New Varieties of Food Grain, Mexico: A Case Study,* Report to the United Nations, in press.
80. *World Energy Supplies 1960–1970.*
81. "Exposicion en la Reunion Continental sobre la Ciencia y il Hombre," *Energia Electrica en America Latina* (Mexico, DF, June 1973).
82. *Ibid.*
83. *Britannica World Atlas.*
84. R. Wilkie, *San Miguel: A Mexican Collective Ejido* (Stanford, Calif.: Stanford University Press, 1971).
85. *Ibid.*
86. Heath et al., *Land Reform and Social Revolution in Bolivia* (New York: Praeger, 1970).
87. *Production Yearbook 1972.*
88. Bruce Netschert et al., *Energy in the American Economy 1850–1975* (Baltimore, Md.: Johns Hopkins Press, 1960).
89. Dawson, *Communist China's Agriculture.*
90. *Production Yearbook 1972.*

Chapter Three

Assessing Rural Energy Needs

How are we to determine how much energy poor rural communities need for development? Projections of energy use are generally made by extrapolating past trends in the use of commercial fuels. They rarely take into account the distribution of energy use among different kinds of consumers, or the levels of use that are needed for a healthy and productive existence; and they usually ignore the fuels which are most important in rural areas—wood, crop residues, and dung. While such projections can serve as a rough proxy for a more detailed examination of energy's role in the industrialized countries, where commercial energy use is widespread and per capita consumption is high, it is not of much value in dealing with the problems and needs of poor countries.

India is one of the few countries to have made some preliminary efforts to assess noncommercial fuel use in the Energy Survey published in 1965. But India shares with other poor nations in a significant failing in evaluating energy needs: projections of fuel use do not systematically include the fuel needed to spur growth in agriculture. The consequence is the neglect of the most important energy policy problems of poor countries, which center around the question of how available capital can be invested in the countryside to provide productive employment and a rapid rate of economic growth.

The Indian government's 1965 report on rural electrification excluded many poor people from its calculations from the start. In discussing growth potential for rural electricity use, the report says:

> For the purpose of assessment of further demand, landless laborers have not been considered relevant as potential customers, partly because of their low economic status and partly because of the type and conditions of their houses.[1]

This was a self-defeating premise on which to base rural electrification policy. Obviously, when income is low, demand or ability to buy food or fuel or necessities of life will be low also. To the free market economist, a "shortage" may not exist if prices rise high enough to curb demand and bring it into balance with supply, but the shortage is real enough for the hungry. Development is concerned with *creating demand* and fulfilling needs. It is therefore important to separate "demand" for essential commodities (in the free market sense of the word) from the *need* for them, and the investment required to fulfill those needs.*

In this chapter, we will attempt to present a method for evaluating energy needs for agricultural development. An actual determination of energy needs depends on a host of physical and economic characteristics of the region such as the amount of land, adequacy and variability of rainfall, depth of underground water, distance from towns, and the like. Nonetheless, the nature of rural energy needs throughout the Third World is similar enough that the method we present here could find widespread applicability. Both theoretical and field research are needed to improve upon the method and numerical estimates described here. Energy needs can be split into three categories:**

1. Domestic energy needs—cooking, heating, and lighting, for example.

2. Energy for agriculture and industry—that is, energy needs for economic growth and the creation of productive employment. Power for irrigation pumps, coke for steel production, or oil for the transportation of essential goods are examples.

3. Energy needs for the provision of essential social services such as education and medical care.

Energy plays a much smaller role in the provision of social services than in the other two categories, and concept of need is also much more a matter of opinion. The amount of money and fuels devoted to "defense" depends on the perception of the threat to security and on prestige. Some schools do use light from sunshine. A small mobile medical unit might provide useful service to 10,000 villagers, while a monumental hospital designed to serve the rich in the city may serve a tenth as many people and use several times more fuel. None of this is meant to denigrate the importance of education or medical care, or domestic water supply and the like; these services are incontestably essential. But their energy cost is usually small when compared to, say, cooking or irrigation. We will therefore deal with these issues only in the context of integrated development.

---

*The Indian government has now accepted this concept in principle at least and has incorporated it into a "minimum needs" program which is a large portion of the Fifth Plan (1974–1979). The program's goals are to provide the poor with a certain minimum standard of living "by social consumption and investment in the form of education, health, nutrition, drinking water, housing, communications and electricity."[2]

**We do not include energy uses for recreation because these are rather small, and *large* expenditures of energy for recreation in poor countries would be extravagances rather than needs.

It must be emphasized that both domestic and developmental energy needs depend not only on the desired work or products but also on the efficiency with which the energy is used. This needs to be stressed because of the widespread and persistent confusion about the relation of economic growth and energy use growth. Production is related not so much to gross energy input into the economy as to the useful work obtained from energy use (Chapter Two) and the composition of the economy.[3] *Economic growth would be tied to growth in energy use only if the composition of the economy and technology were constant.*

But both factors change. Thus, gross per capita energy use in the United States doubled between 1850 and 1950[4]* while per capita GNP increased almost five-fold between 1870 and 1950.[7] This occurred even while the U.S. economy was rapidly shifting from agriculture to industry, which is generally much more energy-intensive.[8]

Greater efficiency of energy use was thus at least as important as greater energy use in increasing the gross national product of the U.S. in the period 1850–1950. Three energy technologies were primarily responsible: the internal combustion engine, the steam engine (and turbine), and the electric generator. These technologies tended to use coal, oil, natural gas, and hydropower more economically than less concentrated sources of energy such as wood; per capita economic growth thus resulted primarily from fuel substitution and only to a lesser extent from total per capita energy growth.

The analysis in this book leads to the conclusion that what is important is an increase in useful work, which must be obtained from a combination of more fuel use, fuel substitution, and an increase in the efficiency of energy resources that are now used.

To define energy needs it is therefore necessary to know how energy is used today (Chapter Two), the capital costs associated with increasing the efficiency of energy use, and the costs associated with increasing the supply of various fuels. We will first discuss the domestic energy sector, and then go on to examine the agricultural sector, interspersed with comments on how these principles might apply to some of the villages and countries described in Chapter Two.

DOMESTIC ENERGY NEEDS

Cooking and heating are the main domestic uses of fuel for people everywhere. Comparing the information gathered by Openshaw in Gambia,[10] and the Energy Survey of India,[11] and the Khadi Village Industries Commission,[12] we find that energy use for cooking in the two countries is about the same. In Gambia about

---

*Draft animals are included. There were about 10 million draft animals (mostly horses) in the U.S. in 1870[5] each probably weighing about 400 to 500 kilograms and consuming 40 to 50 million Btu of energy per year.[6]

55 percent of the woodfuel is used for cooking, 35 percent for heating, and 10 percent for all other uses (primarily ironing). Cooking fuel is an extremely important part of the energy picture in rural areas of the Third World, generally representing about 50 percent of the fuel use in many areas, and perhaps up to 80 percent or 90 percent in the warmer areas, especially where wood is in very short supply, as in the Gangetic plain.

The data from Gambia and India indicate that annual fuel use for cooking with open, slow-burning fires is 5 to 7 million Btu per capita. Because of the low efficiency of such stoves, the fuel use is much higher than in the U.S.A. where the annual per capita use of 3 million Btu for electric stoves (including waste heat at the power plant) and the one to two million Btu for gas stoves without pilot lights.[13] * Approximate data on the use of liquid petroleum gases for cooking in Indian cities indicates an annual cooking energy use of 1 to 1.5 million Btu per capita.[14] To summarize, per capita annual energy needs for cooking vary between 1 and 7 million Btu, depending on the fuel, on the way in which it is burned, on the kinds of cooking vessels used,** and, of course, on the quantity and type of food that is cooked.

Of course, the relative efficiency of fuels for cooking is only one aspect of the energy problem. Whether it is desirable to improve the efficiency of fuel use depends on tangible and intangible economic considerations— primarily capital cost, land availability, soil conservation and flood control, and the opportunity costs of using land to produce fuelwood, and of using dung and crop residues directly as fuels.

Whether wood is readily available and what kind of damage results from extensive wood-cutting are two of the most important factors in evaluating present use of wood as fuel. The soil erosion, the spreading deserts, and vulnerability to floods in deforested areas all over the Third World are clear signals that unplanned use of forest resources can and does have serious adverse consequences.[15] Further, even in countries where woodlands are plentiful, extensive and unplanned use of woodfuel has depleted the capital stock of forests. In Gambia, for example, Openshaw has made the following observations:

> Formerly only dead or dying trees were removed for woodfuel but now living trees are cut and at increasingly greater distances from the villages. In many of the sampled villages, the people complained that woodfuel was more and more difficult to obtain: now the collectors have to set off at mid-day in order to collect and be back for nightfall, whereas previously the woodfuel was just outside the door. Some further ventured the information that it was man's destruction

*Note that *per capita* energy use for cooking tends to *increase* as the number of people per household decreases. In the U.S. the number of people per household is much smaller than in poorer countries.

**Much less energy is needed to cook with pressure cookers than with ordinary pots. A research effort at determining the energy use for cooking with pressure cookers, the costs, and the design of cheaper pressure cookers certainly seems worthwhile.

of the trees that had brought about this situation. All villagers said they would co-operate in tree planting schemes to establish woodfuel plantations provided they were shown the basic skills and there appears to be a real need for village woodlots.[16]

Apparently, an enormous amount of labor is now invested in the collection of fuelwood. Openshaw estimates that the capital costs of establishing village woodlots to supply fuel wood—excluding land costs and the costs of local labor—would be about $20 per hectare. The money would be spent primarily to provide suitable plant varieties and to train villagers to operate the plantations; the investment would be in the local currency. While it may be reasonable to omit the cost of land in areas where it is plentiful (see below), it is not correct to omit the cost of construction labor for schemes which do not yield immediate benefit. Until the woodlots mature the villagers would still have to spend the customary amount of labor for collecting fuel. Openshaw's estimates for large-scale plantations which include the cost of labor run to about $200 per hectare.

Each hectare would have an annual yield of about 15 tons of wood, or enough cooking fuel for 40 to 50 people. The gestation period would vary with the species of tree used for the plantation. For fuelwood plantations in Gambia, Openshaw recommended eucalyptus, or the Indian Neem tree, in which case it would take about 10 years for a plantation to mature. At $5 per ton of wood (30¢ per million Btu) the annual output per hectare would be worth $75. At a discount rate of 10 percent the present worth of all the wood that will be produced from this scheme, starting 10 years from the date of planting, is about $300; the present worth of the capital invested is $120 assuming that $200 is invested in equal installments of $40 over the first five years. The main benefits of the scheme in places like China and Gambia, where felling of live trees is widespread, would probably accrue in terms of soil and water conservation, since, according to Openshaw's estimates, *wood plantations can supply fuel with only one-fifth the land that is used with present practices.* Because of this it is reasonable to omit the cost of land from the estimate of capital cost.

One must also note that the capital cost of replacing wood with petroleum (kerosene) would, in general, cost more than a wood plantation. (This includes the effects of the higher efficiency of oil use. The capital investment required for 1 million Btu per year of oil production, refining, and transport in the U.S. are about $6 to $8.[17]) If the costs of oil exploration, of the special stoves required to burn oil, and of oil transport to the villages are added, then the cost of conserving land by using petroleum instead of wood is seen to be at least twice as large as the cost of village woodlots.

It is important to bear in mind that the availability of land is a necessary element. Where both land and fuel are scarce, as they are in the Gantetic plain, and the same land could be used to cultivate food instead of fuel, the calculation is less simple.

The management of the village woodlot will need special care. There will be temptations of cutting prematurely before the stand is established, or overcutting once it is. If there are many poor people in the village, some will probably harvest wood for illegal sale. These and other problems (such as equitable distribution of the wood, or the allocation of jobs to care for the plantation) must be anticipated and reasonable solutions sought if the investment is to be fruitful. On the plus side, good planning and management of woodlots could permit them to be integrated with long-range national and regional afforestation and soil conservation programs designed to ensure the stability and continuing productivity of tropical soils. The technical aspects of forestry are beyond our competence, but we venture this suggestion as it seems to merit serious study.

Where the supply of land is limited, the problems of supplying fuel for keeping warm are much more difficult because there are so many immediate needs which the limited land and capital resources must fulfill. Energy use for heating in poor countries depends not only on the weather but also on the availability of fuel. Of course, tropical areas, such as the Indian coastal region and South East Asia, need no fuel for keeping warm. But in the Gangetic plain people do suffer from cold weather. A light frost at night is common in the winter,[18] yet there is practically no heating beyond that provided by the cooking fires. In contrast, the use of fuel for heating in Gambia is much larger even though the climate is warmer.

In the cold climates the poor try to keep warm by wearing such clothes as they can garner and by huddling around open fires; in Kashmir, people wear loose clothing and carry a small pot of embers underneath. But the term "space heat," which connotes a well-built house with effective stoves or central heating systems, hardly applies to most of the homes in the Third World.

Whatever the terminology, keeping out the cold is a necessity in many areas of the Third World such as North China, Afghanistan, the Andean, and Himalayan regions and most places south of the Tropic of Capricorn. For example, in the Sao Paulo district of Brazil, there were more than 40 reported cases of death from exposure to cold during a four-week cold spell in 1974.

Warm clothing would immensely improve the lot of poor people who live in such regions. Hot water and soap to wash them with would make them last much longer, for where clothes are washed by beating them against rocks, they wear out quickly. For example, a hand woven cotton shirt costing about $1 may resist only two months of wear if it is washed by beating against stones, but would last much longer if it is washed more gently. A small investment in a solar water heater and a few wooden tubs would greatly extend the life of clothes and help to keep people warm.

Wood is the most common fuel for heating. As noted in Chapter Two, China's afforestation program suffers serious setbacks because fuelwood supply is not a part of the program. Development strategy for cold climates must take into account fuel needs for keeping warm. Where land is at a premium, as in much of China, the pressure on the land could be eased by an integrated plan which includes village woodlots in afforestation programs, improved housing, and installation of efficient wood-burning furnaces, such as downdraft stoves of the Franklin type that were once common in the U.S.A. These could be made with local materials, such as bricks. The capital costs of such a scheme are likely to be high, though local labor and materials and simple, efficient design could reduce them. But the costs of *not* undertaking a sound program to meet these needs are likely to be higher; for when it is cold, people will find the fuel and use it in the most expedient way, making the struggle for soil and water conservation much harder. A shortage of timber is one of the major factors limiting Chinese economic development, in Richardson's opinion.[19] With a furnace costing about $50 to $100 (based on the wholesale price in the U.S.A. of a simple, downdraft cast iron, wood-burning heating-cum-cooking stove), fuel requirements for families living in cold areas of China could be cut in half, thus relieving the country's critical wood shortage. The amount of wood consumed in a reasonably efficient furnace is on the order of 1,500 Btu per house* per hour per degree centigrade difference between the indoor and outdoor temperatures. If we assume that heating fuel must keep the house at about 10°C (50°F)—with clothes providing the warmth above that temperature—then the fuel needs in Northeastern China, where the climate is comparable to that in Minnesota, would be about 50 or 60 million Btu per year, or about 4 tons of wood per family (0.8 tons per capita). This is probably less than half the amount that is presently used. In cold areas where gothermal hot water or volcanic heat is available, it may be cheaper to combine housing programs with the provision of space heat and hot water from gothermal energy rather than wood. This method of heating is common in Iceland. In countries such as Tanzania, where land is plentiful and the climate not as cold, but capital is in short supply, efficient stoves probably cannot be justified since their capital costs are likely to exceed those of village woodlots.

In the northern stretches of the plains of the Ganges and Indus Rivers, the mean winter temperatures are 10°C to 15°C with nighttime temperatures often in the 0 to 10°C range. The forests have long since been cleared. Clothes and quilts stuffed with cotton are the main methods of keeping warm. The lack of forests, the severe and chronic shortages of food, the scarcity of land and abundance of people, the flooding problems that have been caused by deforestation, make the outlook for provision of heating fuel appear dim.

Immediate and sustained increases in the production of food are the paramount need in the Gangetic plain. Much of the misery on this earth is concentrated in that fertile belt of land, which includes Bangladesh and the

---

*We assume a small, well-built house. We do not include the costs associated with the house in this calculation since good housing is an even greater need than space heating.

Indian states of West Bengal, Bihar, and Uttar Pradesh. In an area where almost all the land is devoted to cultivation, it will be difficult, if not impossible, to establish successful woodlots unless the productivity of the land can be increased simultaneously. The village commons, used for pasture, could be used to grow wood, but its use as a village woodlot has to be tied to increases in food for cattle which could come from increases in food (and hence fodder) production and intensive cultivation of cattle feed. In other parts of India, such as hill areas along the coasts, wood is the principal domestic fuel and cow dung is used as manure. Here it should be more feasible to establish village woodlots to supply fuel and help control soil erosion.

There is another related problem. Rural families, particularly those with little or no land, like to have their own cattle because they make use of the "free" grazing land and provide the owners with a source of labor for the fields and transportation, and dung for cooking. The nutrients that these cattle get from the commong grazing land and the fodder are, in large measure, not returned to the soil; thus its productivity is degraded. The current low level of productivity is probably maintained by nitrogen-fixing blue-green algae, some human excrement deposited in the common land, the partial return of dung as the cattle graze and, in some areas, silt deposited by periodic floods. This is another illustration of how rural development problems are bound up with each other.

PEAK LABOR AND SELECTIVE MECHANIZATION

We have noted that one of the most severe problems in agricultural economics all over the world is the peak labor problem—that is, certain operations in the crop cycle, such as transplanting rice, harvesting, threshing, and so on, demand much more labor in a brief period than is ordinarily required for most of the year. In the cultivation of rice in Taiwan, transplanting takes 12 percent of the total annual labor and harvesting another 16 percent,[20] although these two operations together may last less than 30 days. In Chapter Two we noted that the same problem exists in Chinese agriculture and in the villages of Gambia. It exists in the U.S.A., where large numbers of migrant farm workers move with the seasons to where there is peak demand for labor, and still are unemployed for much of the year.

The problem is particularly acute where, for lack of a suitable climate, adequate irrigation, or other farm inputs, only one crop is grown each year. Multiple cropping can increase employment but causes its own peak labor demands, for it puts a premium on quick harvesting and land preparation for sowing the next crop.

The peak labor problem adversely affects rural development in three ways:

1. It causes high unemployment for much of the year and this in turn is a principal reason for the low productivity of labor.

2. It can inhibit the adoption of agricultural innovations particularly in the typical situation, where the small farmer cannot afford to hire the added labor needed at critical times.

3. It leaves many small farmers with little option but to have more children to provide labor for the farm. This requires no capital outlay, but its long-run costs are much larger than those of using animals or machines.

The relation of the labor needs of agriculture to lower birth rates has not, to our knowledge, been empirically studied. Industries and services have no comparable peak labor demands. Therefore, as agricultural population declines— that is, as the productivity of labor in agriculture increases, and peak labor operations are mechanized—and industrial and service employment increases, it would appear that one of the main incentives for having many children is eliminated, since families which obtain their income outside agriculture feel little economic need for having large numbers of children. This means that *a reduction or elimination of the peak labor demand in agriculture could result in a lower birth rate. Moreover, new or additional employment could be in any economic sector—agriculture and related industries, urban industries, or the service sector—as long as the peak labor demand is reduced.* Empirical research on the connection of peak labor demand and the birth rate is desperately needed, for it could have profound implications for development policy.

Peak labor demand can be reduced or eliminated by selective mechanization of those agricultural operations that cause it. This means providing energy to substitute for human labor at these critical times in the crop cycle. The source of energy could be more draft animals, stronger draft animals, or fuels such as oil, biogas, wood, and coal to power machines.

There is, of course, no single prescription for what source of power should be used to reduce peak labor requirements. Conditions vary from one region to the next and from one farmer to the next. Even so, some broad observations should help in making a more detailed analysis of what mix of power sources is appropriate to a particular situation.

In tropical Africa there are large numbers of cattle that are not used for draft purposes. In many areas the cattle are kept to provide essential protein in the form of milk and blood, and occasionally, in the form of meat. Sometimes they are sold for slaughter and provide a source of revenue as well. Many of these cattle could be used to provide power for farms and light irrigation, and in some areas this is being done. The problems are those of introducing new technology into agriculture, providing adequate extension services and, perhaps, overcoming social resistance to the use of cattle for draft purposes.

In India the situation is considerably different. Though much abuse has been heaped on the Indian farmer for his supposedly irrational attitude toward cattle, detailed studies such as the ones by Harris[21] and Odend'hal[22] show that these attitudes are firmly rooted in the economic realities in which the farmer finds himself and that religious belief "derives power and sustenance from the material rewards it confers upon both men and animals."[23] It is also clear from a number of studies that shortages of power on Indian farms are frequent during the busy season (ploughing just after the first rains, for example).[24,25,26] Farmers who do not own enough cattle to plough their own fields cannot rely on borrowing them at the time they need them most. The shortage of power on the farm sometimes inhibits the use of heavier and more effective farm implements such as steel ploughs.

Fodder and pastureland for cattle are often in short supply. For this reason Indian farmers calculate the food budgets of animals with great care, bestowing food and attention on working bullocks or pregnant cows, with the rest left to fend for themselves. Mayer has described this graphically:

> The working bullocks, on whose efficiency cultivation entirely depends, are usually fed with chopped bananas at the time of fodder scarcity. But the milch cows have to live in a semi-starved condition, getting what nutrition they can from grazing on the fields after their rice harvest (Gangulee 1935:17).
>
> At present cattle are fed largely according to the season. During the rainy period they feed upon the grass which springs up on the *uncultivated* hillsides... But in the dry season there is hardly any grass, and cattle wander on the *cropless* lands in an often halfstarved condition. True there is some fodder at these times in the shape of rice straw and dried copra, but it is not generally sufficient, and is furthermore given mainly to the animals actually working at the time. (As quoted in Harris[27]).

Obviously the lot of the Indian bullock and cow is as hard or harder than the lot of the farmer. It seems fair to conclude that, as in many other activities, most Indian farmers make about as thorough use of their cattle as their circumstances permit.

In a few areas of India there may be some grazing land, not suited for intensive agriculture, but which may support some increase in the population of cattle. For many, if not most, areas of India, an increase in bullock power could come from intensive cultivation of cattle feed and from advances in food crop yields which, in general, also increase the supply of fodder for animals (see Chapter Four for a fuller discussion). Mechanizing irrigation would release bullock labor now used for that purpose.[28] This would permit some increase in the power available for tilling, either by way of better fed bullocks or more bullocks or both, since the feed now used to sustain the bullocks which work to irrigate the fields, would be available for other tasks.

From the social or national point of view, it may be more desirable to increase the number of draft animals than to improve the strength of a smaller number of animals (where a choice must be made). This is because a larger animal population affords poorer farmers the opportunity to acquire more cattle for their small farms. Indeed, one of the principal reasons that farmers keep cows alive at a bare subsistence level and feed them as well as possible only during pregnancy and the initial period of lactation is the hope that they will bear male offspring. But the argument for stronger and larger animals is threefold: they can draw better and heavier implements; the protein requirements of draft animals do not increase when they are working;[29] and the marginal efficiency of draft animals is higher than the average efficiency.[30] That is to say, an added Btu fed to an existing animal will result in larger available useful energy than the same calorie fed to a new animal. Thus if food for cattle remains limited, fewer animals could make better use of the energy and protein content of the food now available to them.

Increasing fodder production and in turn feeding a larger animal population is the traditional method in increasing the power on farms in India and other poor countries. This method is slow and cannot be expected to yield the large increases in installed horsepower which are necessary for rapid agricultural growth. In Japan where small mechanized farms are common, the average installed horsepower is 1.6 hp per hectare (Table 2–1, Chapter Two). In many poor countries installed horsepower is little more than a third of this amount.

In India, for example, the 150 million or so draft animals represent an installed power of about 75 million horse power or about 0.6 hp per hectare. An addition of 1/2 to 1 horsepower per hectare to bring Indian farms closer to the Japanese level would mean adding 70 to 140 million horsepower which is needed to fulfill the power needs of India's farms (excluding irrigation—see the following sections). This is beyond the potential for expanding draft animal population in the next decade.

It appears, therefore, that to make more power generally available to farms in many poor countries a combination of elements is required: more intensive use of grazing land, limited increases in cattle population (when feasible), and farm machines. We reemphasize that rapid increases in food production result in large increases in crop residues and that these residues can be used as fodder to support both stronger and more draft animals.

Small farm machines similar to the walking tractors* in common use in Japan and Taiwan are clearly called for in India and in many parts of Asia (e.g., China) and Latin America, where a similar dearth of power is evident.

---

*Elimination of the cab and a simpler construction reduces the weight of the tractor, thereby increasing its energy efficiency. It also reduces the capital cost.

These same engines can, in many instances, be used for irrigation and small-scale industries.

The principal policy problems connected with introducing farm machines have to do with their capital requirements and employment effects.

CAPITAL REQUIREMENTS

Individual plots of land in the Third World are small—often one hectare or less. This makes it difficult for the small farmer to purchase farm machinery, for even one small tractor (5 to 15 horsepower) suffices for many small farms. Therefore, small farmers can neither get loans for purchasing machines nor use them profitably if they have the means to buy them—even though the capital cost per horsepower of a small tractor is $20 to $30 compared to $50 to $100 for a pair of bullocks.*

A simple comparison of tractors with draft animals on the basis of capital cost would be misleading, even apart from the questions of access to the services of machines (discussed in the next two sections).

In addition to working in the fields, bullocks, horses, and mules provide power for transportation, some irrigation and, in many parts of India, they provide cooking fuel in the form of dung. However, mechanical power is nearly always required to exploit the potential of underground water for irrigation and multiple cropping. Aninal and human labor is insufficient for anything but light irrigation to supplement rains. Therefore, the cost of selective mechanization and mechanical irrigation using different combinations of draft animals, farm machines, engine-operated pumps, or electric pumps will vary greatly with the area under consideration.

Decreasing peak labor requirements will not by itself produce more food. The equipment cannot pay for itself unless other capital investments in other areas are made simultaneously. Irrigation is by far the most capital-intensive of these investments; it requires anywhere from $100 to $1,000 or more per hectare.[32, 33] The lower end of this range applies to small-scale projects such as persian wheels, tubewells, and tanks; the higher end to large dams with long canals (including interest during construction, which greatly increases the cost of many large-scale projects which take 10 years or more before they yield any benefits). Still more capital is required for the power required to pump the water. Even assuming the low end of all these estimates—$20 per hectare for farm machines, $100 per hectare for tubewell irrigation, and $200 per hectare

*Engines usually have limited overload capability. In this respect draft animals are superior to machines because an animal with an average output of 1 horsepower is capable of delivering many times that for one or two minutes.[31] Therefore, in some cases it may not be possible to reduce the size of small tractors because the peak power requirements of some field operations may be several horsepower.

for the power facilities,* a conventional development scheme would require at least $320 per hectare.

Undertaking such a scheme on three-fourths of India's cultivated land would require $32 billion or about six times the total annual governmental expenditure. Of course, not all irrigation projects will be as cheap as $100 per hectare. The requirements of flood control, the dearth of underground water, the need to exploit hydropower resources will dictate that in many areas medium and large-scale works are more appropriate. In addition, these agricultural development works require large investments in industries, in roads and railways, in fuel production, in cities and market towns, to say nothing of other essential expenditures on health, education, and the like. India, like many other countries, is truly short of development capital and every effort must be made to spend it as effectively as possible.

REDUCING CAPITAL COSTS

Costs depend principally on the choice of technology and on the way the equipment is designed and used. For example, the capital costs for a compost pit are lower than those for a chemical fertilizer plant, and different kinds of irrigation projects and farm machines differ greatly in cost. Treated bamboo or baked clay pipes may be cheaper than steel pipes.** Of course, the choices are not always mutually exclusive and different conditions demand different projects and equipment. However, as we have shown, even the relatively cheap farm machines and tubewell irrigation can be beyond the reach of poor countries.

This situation arises partly because development schemes usually make poor use of capital equipment. The electric motor attached to an irrigation pump is used only when the pump is operating—usually less than 20 percent of the time. The engine in the tractor usually sits idle when the tractor chassis does—or about 90 percent of the time. Irrigation pumps are switched on at any time during the peak season and, together with the air conditioning in government offices and luxury hotels, creates peak demands on expensive electric generating capacity. This is the machine equivalent of the peak labor problem.

To reduce capital costs, equipment and its most expensive parts can be designed to be used in as many essential applications as feasible, so that idle

---

*This assumes an installed power requirement of about 1 horsepower per hectare. This figure, of course, varies enormously from one place to the next, because of the different water requirements, water table depths, etc.

**Baked clay pipes are currently used in some areas of South India.[34] Bamboo pipes are also used, but they tend to deteriorate with exposure to water and sunshine and cannot withstand high pressures. Research on treating bamboo pipes to retard deterioration and improve their strength could yield handsome dividends.

time is reduced as much as possible. For example, when the engine of a tractor or mechanized rice transplanter is not being used in the fields, it should be used to pump water (as is often done in Punjab, for example) or haul a trailer with surplus agricultural produce to a nearby market town.

Electrified irrigation systems, crop processing, and small-scale industries should be designed to minimize the installed electric generating capacity for a given consumption of electricity. Drip irrigation (the method of delivering a continuous supply of water to plants through small holes punched in the pipe), while requiring higher unit investment for distributing water to the fields, may reduce overall capital costs by keeping irrigation water needs to a minimum (since water is absorbed better when it is delivered in small continuous doses). This method can reduce the number of wells required to irrigate the land and, possibly, the power to pump the water.

When the electric motors that drive irrigation pumps are not being used for irrigation, they could power grain-milling machines, sugarcane crushers, oil pressers, or small-scale industries such as cotton, spinning, and weaving. This approach would cut the capital cost of equipment, make feasible some development schemes which are now impractical because of their high capital cost, and create more economic opportunities in the villages.

The capital equipment that already exists in underdeveloped countries can also be used more productively. Pumps can be installed in existing wells to provide a more copious supply of water for irrigation. Electric power plants in underdeveloped countries operate at low capacity factors:* 40 percent is typical and lower capacity factors are not uncommon.[35] Improving this capacity factor by making more complete use of installed equipment in agriculture, as suggested above, and in industry could reduce the needs for capital in this essential but capital-intensive sector.

Industries such as paper and petrochemicals that use large quantities of low- to medium-grade steam, could install both electric generators and high-pressure steam turbines to produce electricity and the requisite grade of process steam together, thus saving fuel and reducing the capital requirements of new industries.[35, 36] In many instances the total annual operating costs of existing industrial installations that use oil could be markedly reduced.[37] Automobile factories could cut back production of cars and turn out more tractors and farm implements. Private automobiles and motorcycles, which lie idle perhaps 95 percent of the time, are a luxury which, with appropriate modifications, could be put to more effective use as tractors, irrigation engines, and transport vehicles for food and fertilizers.

In the United States 6 million automobiles are junked each year and sold for scrap at $30 a ton. With some fixing up, many of the engines could be used in industry and in small power plants to drive generators in villages and

---

*Capacity factor is defined here as the proportion of a plant's capacity that is actually in use averaged over one year.

small towns. While the costs of transporting an auto engine (and other usable parts) from the U.S. to Africa, Asia, or Latin America may be high—perhaps several hundred dollars—a 100 horsepower engine at $15 per horsepower would be worth $1,500. This concept can be extended to include all manner of valuable equipment from cooking ranges and refrigerators to hospital equipment now discarded in the industrialized nations because labor there is too expensive to service it. A comprehensive effort should be undertaken immediately to evaluate the problems (e.g., spare parts) and potential of such transfers of capital equipment. This appears to be an avenue of reducing the capital costs of development that has not yet been systematically explored.

A major policy implication of the approach outlined here is that only integrated development programs can accomplish rural development at minimum capital cost. Obviously, machines cannot be designed for multiple applications if one doesn't know what the specific applications will be. Moreover, if versatile machines are designed, but then put to use for one purpose only, the end result will be higher, not lower, capital cost. Birth control programs this year, irrigation the next, domestic water supply the year after that, and farm machines 10 years later will not effectively cut capital costs. The compartmentalized approach may be suited to the empire building that politicians and bureaucrats the world over engage in, but it will not bring about rapid development. Some urgently needed efforts, such as afforestation schemes and many irrigation projects, can take effect even in the absence of an integrated development plan. Lack of a plan is no excuse for delay in beginning these programs.

MECHANIZATION AND EMPLOYMENT POLICY

Mechanization has important implications for the job opportunities available to the landless, the land renters, sharecroppers and the owners of very small plots of land who must have jobs outside their own land to make ends meet. The demand for peak labor is probably the only important leverage the poorest and most powerless people have in village societies. Villages are dominated by the landowners who not only control the most important physical resource—land—but are also often in the majority. Obviously, most of these landowners are poor themselves but not as poor and vulnerable as the landless.

Farm machines whose only purpose is to eliminate peak labor demands will deprive the poorest people of their only source of economic power. With the continuing strong pressure on food and money supply because of population growth and inflation, it is likely that the landless will be denied food, that they will migrate to the cities *en masse* in search of it, and die because they won't find it. The current large-scale migrations to the cities by poor villagers of India and Bangladesh hunting in vain for food are a clear signal that the starving out of the landless is not an academic speculation.

As peak labor requirements in agriculture are reduced, more job opportunities *must* be created. This can be done by multiple cropping, public works that create productive assets such as dams and roads, collection and processing of local fuels, the development of market towns, and effective use of capital equipment by all.

The creation of such opportunities for the poor in villages cannot be left to chance or the good will of the more powerful segments of rural society. Raj Krishna has made the following observations on the minimum needs program in India which is part of the current (fifth) five-year plan:

> In view of past experience the proposal to pump Rs. 11,000 crores [a total of $14 billion over five years] for works in the rural areas evokes the grave anxiety that if the quality of a large number of local projects is as bad as it has been, and the leakage of funds due to corruption is as great as it has been, there may be neither a substantial addition to productive capacity nor a significant income transfer to show for the enormous outlay. Instead of reducing the poverty and idleness of the poorest, it may further enrich the rural oligarchy and bureaucracy, and increase inequity and tension in the countryside. Therefore, two critical requirements of the success of a massive works programme are: a radical restructuring of the district development administration, and a radical politicisation of the under-employed rural proletariat. Strong and well-staffed Project Formulation Bureaus must be established in every district to prepare shelves of technically and economically sound local projects. Recognized private consultancy firms can also be mobilized for this task. And the unemployed, the landless, the crop-sharers and the insecure tenants must be organized into militant unions to demand that project funds and benefits really reach the poorest and are not swallowed by contractors, rich farmers and petty bureaucrats through whom they are channelled. Incidentally, these unions should also demand that land reform laws be implemented within specified periods of time, and that in the distribution of credit and inputs, the small and marginal farmers receive fixed minimum quotas. Without militant rural unionism, laws and policies have not benefited and will not benefit the mass of the rural proletariat. I would even suggest that the Government should subsidize the organization of rural unions—regardless of the nature of the parties who organize them—in proportion to the certified membership of each union.
>
> The work guarantee principle will have to be built into the works programme in one region after another as the capacity to implement large shelves of local projects grows. There are two fundamental ethical reasons in support of the "right to work." First, the existence of unemployment of the order of 9 percent of the labour force is not a failure of the working class but a failure of society as a whole

for which the workers suffer. They must receive compensation for this suffering, along with an opportunity to work with self-respect. Second, if the right to property is constitutionally protected, subject to some restrictions, there is no reason why the right to work should not be similarly protected. *Property and work are both desired as durable sources of income; and if one source of income, which the propertied classes have, is protected, there is no reason why the other source of income which the propertyless have is not protected* [emphasis added].[38]

Public works programs must be designed to create productive assets, particularly those which will increase agricultural production, or facilitate its storage and distribution (roads). As a specific example, we illustrate how the use of some of the funds of India's minimum needs program could be used.

It has been estimated that irrigation works in India require an investment of $3 per man day of labor.[39] The capital outlay per man day for minor irrigation works such as wells and tanks is probably lower. Land reclamation, minor irrigation, soil conservation, and road construction alone can probably absorb about 6 million man years of labor during India's 1974–1979 fifth five-year plan. Minor irrigation works alone would create irrigation facilities for 14 million hectares of land. If we assume that irrigation works take about half the total labor for the four activities listed above, the total investment required over five years to irrigate 14 million hectares would be about $2 billion. Of this, $240 million or so could be in the form of food payments to workers (equivalent to 1.2 million tons of wheat at 1974 world prices, or about 1.2 percent of India's current food grain production). This in turn could create roughly 3 million permanent jobs in agriculture and increase annual food production by approximately 5 million tons.*

In the Punjab-Haryana region of India, where the use of high-yielding wheat varieties, irrigation, fertilizers, and pesticides immensely improved the lot of the average farmer, unemployment decreased in spite of rapid mechanization because of the very rapid growth of agricultural production (particularly wheat) following the introduction of the high-yielding seeds.[41] But Raj Krishna has shown that unless agricultural growth is rapid (more than 5 percent per year), the rate of mechanization of threshing can cause unemployment to increase.[42] ** The rate of mechanization in agriculture, particularly for threshing, should be

*Raj Krishna estimates that irrigation works in India result in net increase in employment of 51 man days per hectare.[40] The potential is greater because only 20 percent of India's irrigated land is now cropped more than once. The estimate of increased food production from minor irrigation works has been derived from the estimates for Uttar Pradesh (on the Gangetic Plain) made for the third five-year plan as quoted by Etienne (note 25).

**Note that unemployment will increase as long as the rate at which new jobs are created and filled is less than the rate of growth of the labor force. Thus both employment and unemployment can increase simultaneously.

consistent not only with the needs of increasing production, but also with the capacity of the rest of the economy, including public works programs, to absorb the displaced labor.

In many countries, farmers with small and medium holdings (1 to 5 hectares) control most of the land and constitute the majority of the rural population. These farmers need liberal extension of enough credit to buy farm machines, or bullocks, and to dig private wells to suit their needs; agricultural extension services; and timely provision of suitable seeds, fertilizers and materials to build channels for water or wells, and often this kind of help is sufficient enough to ensure rapid progress.[43] However, many small farmers cannot offer enough collateral to get the loans they need for these purposes. Many small farmers could not make full use of a tubewell or a tractor or a pair of strong bullocks which may still be essential on a part-time basis to improve the productivity of their land. There is, therefore, a need for the government to own and operate tractors, tubewells, fuel and power production and distribution systems (both centralized *and* decentralized) and the like, so that small farmers can have access to them. With such an ownership scheme, the general principle of equipment designed for multiple use has great potential. Such equipment can be used to increase agricultural production *and simultaneously* to create employment for the landless.*

Custom farming, in which irrigation water and farm machine services are provided to farmers by private individuals who own the equipment, is another way of providing these services to small farmers. If the custom farming approach has the advantage that privately owned equipment is likely to be better maintained and more profitably used than state-owned equipment, it has the disadvantage that the services may not be made available to small farmers on terms they can afford. Private loans from moneylenders in India often carry interest rates as high as 36 percent a year.[44] Thus any widespread promotion of the custom farming approach must be accompanied by adequate regulation to ensure that small farmers get their due.

Within this general framework, we can set forth the specific energy needs of agricultural development.

ENERGY NEEDS OF AGRICULTURE

Decreasing peak labor requirements will probably require a few hundred hours of machine use per hectare and a power requirement of 1/2 to 1 horsepower. This implies an energy use on the order of 1 to 3 million Btu per hectare per crop (in addition to animal labor). With high-yielding varieties of wheat and rice threshing often causes a greater peak labor demand, as energy requirements for

---

*The implement used will depend on the crop. It could, for example, be a rice transplanting machine, or harvestor, a mechanical thresher, or a sugarcane crushing machine.

threshing depend on the amount of grain produced per hectare, rather than the amount of land cultivated.

Energy requirements for irrigation and drainage vary a great deal from one region to the next. Indeed, if rainfall is regular and a cold climate permits only one crop a year, irrigation may not be necessary at all. For example, only 3 percent of U.S. corn fields are irrigated.[45] This situation does not apply to most underdeveloped countries where rainfall is generally irregular, occurring mostly during a single three or four month rainy season and where warm climates permit planting many crops a year, given a regular water supply. Moreover, the high-yielding grain varieties require the application of water at the proper time and generally tolerate less variation than the traditional varieties. With few exceptions, irrigation is necessary to increase yields, stabilize food production (that is, decrease yearly fluctuations in yields), and produce several crops a year.*

Gravity irrigation, in which water flowing downhill is channeled onto terraces on the hills, and artesian wells, in which underground water is brought to the surface by the pressure of the layer(s) of rock above it, require little or no mechanical energy. Where the water table is near the surface, as it is in the Gangetic plain and many other areas, the required useful energy may be on the order of 1/2 million Btu per hectare per crop. This may increase to 5 million Btu/ha./crop or more (useful energy) in arid areas with deep water tables, or canal works where water has to be pumped up hills.** For example, it would require large amounts of energy to pump the waters from the Gangetic plain onto the Deccan plateau in South India, or the waters of Lake Victoria up to the Tanzanian plateau.

Since underground water is available close to the surface in the Gangetic plain, the useful energy requirements there would be about 1/2 million Btu/ha./crop. This means a total useful energy requirement of 150 million Btu for Mangaon's 300 hectares. A month's useful energy output of *all* the draft cattle and *half* the humans in Mangaon would be 35 to 40 million Btu, using an optimistic efficiency estimate of 5 percent (Appendix A). Cattle would contribute about 85 percent of this total.

As a practical matter, the useful energy which could be realized from animals and humans at the beginning of a development effort is likely to be much smaller than this estimate, since not all draft cattle and people in the village could be spared for one task, and shortages of food and fodder would limit the work that people and animals could do. The work output of draft

*Current research on seed varieties that will produce high yields without irrigation will, if fruitful, reduce the need for irrigation. But present needs for increased food production and hence for irrigation are too great to wait for the fruition of long-term research, which is often uncertain.

**Irrigation energy requirements vary, of course, with the crop and the rainfall during the time it is planted. This discussion is illustrative of irrigation energy requirements under the various conditions described in Chapter Two.

animals and humans can be increased somewhat as more food and fodder became available—that is, as agricultural production increases. But such increases in work output are not likely to come near meeting the energy requirements of lift irrigation. However, if irrigation water cannot be provided by other means, or if the water requirements are small, then providing light irrigation with draft animals and human labor would at least help to supplement rains and ensure one productive crop a year during the monsoon season.

Fixed nitrogen* can be provided to the soil in four ways: (a) applying chemical nigrogen; (b) applying organic nitrogen from agricultural, animal and human wastes; (c) planting legumes which harbor nitrogen-fixing bacteria in their roots (e.g., soybeans, pulses); (d) seeding the soil with nitrogen-fixing bacteria grown in cultures outside the soil.

We have only scanty information on the last method, but apparently it works in a manner similar to rotating crops with legumes.[46] Organic wastes, except when they come from leguminous plants, do not increase the stock of fixed nitrogen, but return to the soil the nitrogen that the crops absorbed from it. Chemical nitrogen and legumes do increase the stock of fixed nitrogen because, in each case, free nitrogen derived from the atmosphere is fixed (by chemical and biological processes, respectively).

The return of organic fertilizers to the soil is important because it is relatively cheap. Without it, large doses of chemical fertilizers must be added, and even if legumes are planted to fix nitrogen, phosphorous, potassium, and other trace minerals must be added to maintain the productivity of the soil.** Complete recycling of nutrients is, of course, not possible and *some external source of nutrients is usually necessary, particularly if several crops are planted.*

Legumes are important sources of protein in poor countries, and multiple cropping with one or more legume crops each year would accomplish the dual purpose of increasing the supply of protein and fixing nitrogen in the soil. It is also important to note that legumes not only enrich the soil with nitrogen but make additional fuel and fertilizer available in the form of the crop residues. Thus in Peipan (China) each hectare planted with soybeans produces almost three tons of crop residues with an energy value of about 40 million Btu and a nitrogen content of about 10 kg. In addition, each hectare yields 70 kg. of nitrogen (in the form of protein) in the soybeans. If the soybeans are consumed locally, then most of the nitrogen reappears in urine and feces, while some of it

*We will not discuss the energy requirements for potassium and phosphorous fertilizers and pesticides, since they are much smaller than those for chemical nitrogen. The capital requirements for phosphorous and potassium fertilizers are also comparatively small since they are available in natural deposits and the quantities necessary for most crops are smaller than those of nitrogen.

**Significant quantities of trace minerals, particularly phosphorous and lime (calcium) are available in the bones of animal carcasses and in fish scrap. The use of ashes left over from burning wood, crop residues, and dung would also enrich the soil with potassium (about 5 percent) and smaller amounts of other nutrients. This method of soil fertilization has been practiced in China and Japan for centuries.[47]

is retained to provide for the growth of children.* Thus, careful management of human excrement can result in a substantial increase in the stock of fixed nitrogen in an agricultural economy where legumes are grown. In China such management has enabled the soil to be cultivated without loss of productivity for thousands of years. Not long ago, it was common for Chinese farmers to pay gold for human excrement collected in the cities.[49]

The safe return of human feces and urine to the fields is important not only for their fertilizer potential but also crucial to the improvement of sanitary conditions in rural areas, and hence the health of rural people. For example, in many rural areas of Egypt schistosomiasis, a debilitating blood fluke disease acquired primarily through contact with infected water, affects half the people.[50] Its control depends primarily on the sanitary disposal of human feces and urine which, for lack of suitable facilities, are now discharged along the banks of rivers and canals. In Chapter Four we shall see that the investment in latrines necessary to control the disease can also be productively used for providing fertilizers and fuel, thus increasing the benefits of irrigation canals to farming. Considering the enormous cost of the disease in terms of lost labor and agricultural production, as well as the direct costs of controlling the disease, one could even conceive of payments to people to use latrines.

The fertilizer potential of organic wastes can be exploited either by composting (fermentation in the presence of air) or by anaerobic fermentation. Composting results in a complete loss of the fuel value of the wastes, since the bacteria convert the carbon to carbon dioxide, and some of the nitrogen in volitile form (ammonia) escapes to the atmosphere. Anaerobic fermentation, or biogasification, produces the gaseous fuel methane from organic wastes, with no significant loss of fertilizer value. It requires a higher capital investment than composting, but as we shall see in Chapter Four, fuel and electricity produced from the fuel would in many cases be considerably cheaper than that provided by present methods of centralized generation and rural distribution lines. If a biogasification system is not economically feasible, then composting should be encouraged to recycle nutrients to the soil. Of course, composting is already in common practice in many countries, but in many others, such as Tanzania, it is not.

Chemical nitrogen is the most energy-intensive form of fertilizer and the most expensive. The average U.S. price of urea (46 percent nitrogen) rose from about $100 a ton in September 1973 to around $255 a ton—or about $550/ton of contained nitrogen.[51] It is even more expensive for the many countries that import chemical nitrogen from the U.S. since one must add transport costs and the fact that the fertilizers must be paid for in scarce foreign

---

*The nitrogen excreted by humans varies from a low of 4 grams per day when the diet is low in nitrogen (protein) to 18 grams per day when the diet is nitrogen rich (high in protein). Most of the nitrogen appears in the urine in the form of urea. An intake of 50 grams of protein per day (average in many countries) by an adult in nitrogen balance will result in the excretion of about 8 grams of nitrogen per day.[48]

exchange. It takes 75 million Btu to produce a ton of nitrogen from natural gas, and 100 or more million Btu if it is produced from oil and coal, as it is in India. The cost of the fuel alone is around $150 to $200 in most places. (The cost of producing chemical nitrogen is much lower in the U.S. where it is produced from relatively cheap natural gas.) Unless world oil prices decline substantially—and the prospects for that seem dim—it is unlikely that world prices for chemical nitrogen will fall below $300/ton in the next few years. Indeed, the current shortage of manufacturing capacity and high demand for chemical nitrogen, and the high rates of inflation worldwide make it likely that the price will go up before it comes down. Expansion of manufacturing capacity, particularly in the Persian Gulf countries where surplus natural gas is plentiful, would reduce the *cost* substantially, but one cannot predict that a simultaneous reduction in *price* would follow in view of the 1973–74 explosion in oil prices. For most countries, most of this cost will be in foreign exchange. And it will take still further expenditures to deliver the fertilizer to the villages.

The continued use of chemical fertilizers is crucial to maintaining the gains in food production of recent years as a result of the use of high-yielding seeds. Yet short-term increases in fertilizer supply from the industrialized nations will not be forthcoming due to a shortage of fertilizer plant capacity. As noted, India has an installed capacity of around 2 million tons of nitrogen a year, but produces only about 1 million tons and has the potential of rapidly expanding its production of chemical nitrogen. But most other countries are not so fortunate.

Chemical fertilizers are important in conjunction with organic fertilizers for several reasons. First, nutrients which are lost by leaching,* volatilization, and necessarily imperfect recycling must be replaced by chemical fertilizers, except in the case of fixed nitrogen where nitrogen fixing bacteria (either from legume plants or from industrially-grown bacteria) can fill part of the gap. Second, in most cases organic fertilizers cannot immediately provide enough nutrients for high-yielding grain varieties (Table 4–5, Chapter Four). Third, high-yielding grain varieties demand nutrients in precise combinations. Organic methods will not produce these exact combinations. Chemical fertilizers are necessary to give the plants the balanced supply of nutrients they require.

The exact requirements for chemical nitrogen will vary with the variety of seeds used and with the number and variety of crops. If two grains, rice and wheat for example, and one legume such as peas, are planted each year (three crops are feasible in many cases) the chemical nitrogen requirements are likely to be high, perhaps on the order of 100 kg. per hectare per year. In

---

*In many tropical and semitropical areas the water hyacinth has caused serious problems, clogging canals and waterways. It absorbs nutrients leached from the soil into the water and is one of the most efficient plant converters of solar energy, producing up to 200 tons of dry matter per hectare per year. The use of the water hyacinths as a source of fuel, or in compost pits (along with other organic material), and perhaps, in biogas plants could convert this plant pest into a useful resource (see Chapter Four and Appendix B).

addition, smaller amounts of phosphorous, potassium, magnesium, calcium and sulphur would be required, the quantities being determined by the seed varieties, soil characteristics, rainfall, and drainage, and the composition of the organic fertilizers returned to the soil. It would take about 7.5 million Btu to manufacture 100 kg. of nitrogen so that growing three crops a year in Mangaon would require roughly as much energy for chemical fertilizers as would be needed for lift irrigation. In other areas where the water is deeper underground, fuel energy requirements for lift irrigation would probably predominate. The capital investment required to produce 100 kg. of chemical nitrogen annually in a large-scale plant is about $40. Most, perhaps all, of this capital could be generated within an expanding agricultural sector.

There are three other areas where significant amounts of energy are needed for agricultural development: (a) development of market towns (including the requisite services and industries); (b) manufacture of the capital goods for agriculture in large-scale industries; (c) transportation of surplus agricultural produce to cities and towns.*

In the case of market towns and cities, energy is needed not only for the industry and commerce that serve the villagers but also for direct (domestic) and indirect (commercial, transport, and industrial) uses to satisfy the requirements of people who live in the towns and cities.

The energy needs of market towns and cities will depend primarily on the climate, transportation distances and methods, and the mix of industries. Detailed studies must be carried out for each country to determine what these energy needs are and how they can be met. We can get an inkling of the diversity of the conditions by noting that in many African towns wood and charcoal are the principal cooking fuels, whereas in fuel-short North India, many people have to wait in long lines for their small rations of expensive kerosene. Nevertheless analysis in the urban sector should be somewhat easier because more data are available.

The energy required to manufacture the capital goods needed for agriculture can be approximately estimated. The cost of finished steel-based goods (engines, for example) is roughly $5 per kilogram, while it is about $10 per kilogram for electrical goods such as motors and generators. Thus if the investment per hectare in pumps, tractors, engines, and so on is around $200 (exclusive of energy supply) the equivalent weight of steel would be about 40 kilograms. (Other materials would also be required, but we use this steel equivalent to obtain an order of magnitude estimate of the energy investment.) It takes about 70 million Btu to produce one ton of finished steel goods.[52] Thus the energy investment in the capital goods for agriculture would be around

---

*The transportation energy requirements for bringing capital goods to villages would be small by comparison since these goods usually have a high value per unit weight and must be transported only once in many years. The quantities of fertilizers and pesticides which must be transported each year would be relatively small compared to the volume of food moved.

3 million Btu per hectare. This energy investment can be reduced not only by putting a single piece of equipment to many uses but also by incorporating many economical energy conservation methods in both new and existing plants. For example, the energy consumed to make a ton of steel ingots can be economically reduced by about one-third, and similar achievement is possible in many other industries such as cement, paper, and so on, with technology that is available today.[53]

Some rather heavy energy investments are also needed to manufacture the energy supply facilities. Current design of village size biogas plants (capacity 1 billion Btu per year), for example, require 8 kilograms of steel and 20 kilograms of cement (requiring an energy investment of 700,000 to 750,000 Btu) per million Btu per year of capacity.[54] If 10 to 15 million Btu per year are needed to work one hectare of land, the required energy investment to build the biogas plant for each hectare supplied with fuel would be 7.5 to 10 million Btu. The total energy investment in capital goods per hectare (irrigation pumps, farm machines and the biogas plant) is thus comparable to the annual energy requirements needed to work one hectare of land. This relationship will, of course, vary depending on the amount of time the equipment is actually used. While this energy investment in capital equipment is quite small compared to the total energy consumed over the life of the energy consuming equipment (20 or 30 years), the energy requirements during a period of rapid growth may be quite large. We illustrate with a hypothetical example. To introduce this package of capital goods (farm machines, irrigation pumps and tube wells, biogas plants) on 10 million hectares of cultivated land per year (or roughly 10 percent of the cultivated land not now irrigated) would require approximately one-tenth of one quadrillion Btu (10^{14} Btu) per year or about 3 percent of India's current commercial energy use. During the second year of such a program the energy use by the machines installed in the first year would about equal the energy required to manufacture the equipment. After 10 years, however, the annual energy use of all the tractors and pumps in the field would be 10 times higher than the energy use in the manufacturing industry to equip another 10 million hectares.

The heavy demands that such a (hypothetical) program would make on India's steel and cement production* make it imperative that the use of these materials be reduced so far as practicable. For example, a recent analysis of the current designs of biogas plants, showed that these designs are wasteful of materials,[55] and concluded that a reduction of more than 50 percent is possible in the steel and cement required to build biogas plants (see Appendix B for further details).

---

*Roughly 1.5 million tons of steel and 2 to 3 million tons of cement per year, or roughly 25 percent and 20 percent, respectively, of India's annual production of these commodities.

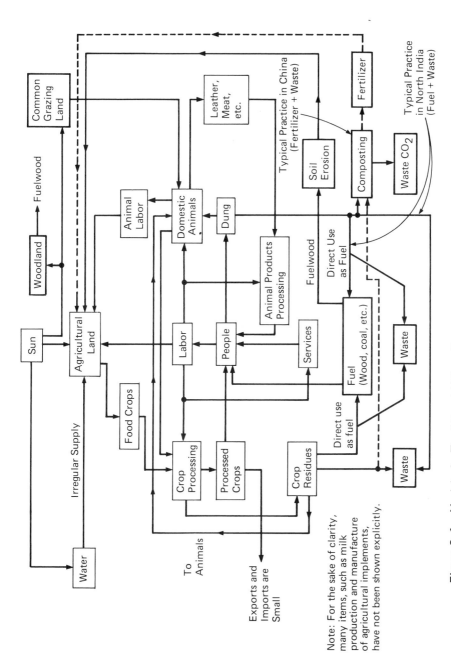

Figure 3-1. Model of a Traditional Village Economy

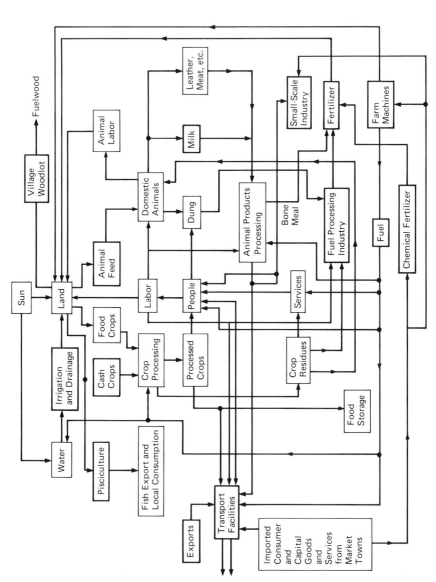

Figure 3-2.   Model of a Developing Village Economy

ECONOMIC MODELS

The many interrelated problems of agricultural development that we have discussed, and some that we have not discussed only because their energy implications are minor, require that we view the agricultural economy as an evolving system. Figure 3–1 shows a flow diagram of the major economic features of a traditional village economy. Figure 3–2 illustrates a developing village economy.

In the traditional village economy, the crops barely provide for the food needs of people and the fodder for the cattle. The rate of growth in the stock of capital goods is small. The energy needs are met by the use of wood and crop residues and, in India, dung. The useful work obtained is small and is inadequate to fuel rapid agricultural growth. The cattle eat crop residues and graze freely on common land. In comparison to the need, the draft animals yield little useful work, and milk animals, little milk.

By contrast, a developing village economy exports a large proportion of its food production and imports capital goods, fertilizers, and consumer goods. The availability of sufficient energy plays a crucial role in such an economy. The main differences between the two flow diagrams are signified by heavy boxes and lines.

Conventional economic models that deal with land, labor, capital, savings, and so on need to be combined with physical or resource models such as the ones illustrated here. Developing both micro and macro models of this kind would be an immensely useful tool in understanding the potential for development and in the design of integrated development efforts. We will illustrate, in a rather simplified way, the application of this integrated technical-economic approach at the end of Chapter Four.

Notes to Chapter Three

1. Planning Commission, *Report on Evaluation of the Rural Electrification Programme* (New Delhi: Government of India, 1965).
2. Planning Commission, *Approach to the Fifth Plan* (New Delhi: Government of India, 1973), p. 9.
3. Energy Policy Project, *A Time to Choose: America's Energy Future* (Cambridge, Mass.: Ballinger Publishing Company, 1974).
4. Bruce Netschert et al., *Energy in the American Economy, 1850–1975* (Baltimore, Md.: Johns Hopkins Press, 1960).
5. *U. S. Cattle and Livestock Statistics* (Washington, D.C.: U.S. Department of Agriculture, n.d.).
6. F. B. Morrisson, *Feeds and Feeding* (Ithaca, N.Y.: Morrisson Publishing Company, 1947).

7. *Long Term Economic Growth, 1860–1970* (Washington, D.C.: U. S. Bureau of Economic Analysis, U. S. Department of Commerce, 1973).

8. Robert H. Williams (ed.), *The Energy Conservation Papers* (Cambridge, Mass.: Ballinger Publishing Company, 1975).

9. Keith Openshaw, "The Gambia: A Wood Consumption Survey and Timber Trend Study, 1973–2000," Unpublished report to the ORA/6RD Gambia Land Resources Development Project, Midlothian, Great Britain, 1973.

10. Keith Openshaw, "Projections of Wood Use in Tanzania," Unpublished report to the Public Works Department, Tanzania, Midlothian, Great Britain, 1973.

11. *Report of the Energy Survey of India Committee* (New Delhi: Government of India, 1965).

12. Khadi Village Industries Commission, "Gobar Gas—Why and How," Bombay, n.d.

13. Energy Policy Project, *A Time to Choose.*

14. O. P. Kharabanda, Larsen and Toubro Limited, Bombay, India, private communication, 1973.

15. R. F. Dasmann et al., *Ecological Principles of Economical Development* (London: John Wiley & Sons Ltd., 1973).

16. Openshaw, "The Gambia," p. 43.

17. J. Hass, *Financing the Energy Industry* (Cambridge, Mass.: Ballinger Publishing Company, 1974).

18. Dudley Stamp, *Asia* (New York: E. P. Dutton & Co., 1958).

19. S. D. Richardson, *Forestry in Communist China* (Baltimore, Md.: Johns Hopkins Press, 1966).

20. You-Tsao Wang, "Farm Mechanization in Taiwan: Its Problems and Research Needs," in H. Southworth (ed.), *Farm Mechanization in East Asia* (New York: Agricultural Development Council, 1972).

21. Marvin Harris, "The Cultural Ecology of India's Sacred Cattle," *Current Anthropology* 7 (1966).

22. Stewart Odend'hal, "Energetics of Indian Cattle in Their Environment," *Human Ecology* 1 (1972).

23. Harris, "The Cultural Ecology."

24. *Ibid.*

25. Gilbert Etienne, *Studies in Indian Agriculture* (Berkeley: University of California Press, 1968).

26. J. Mellor et al., *Developing Rural India* (Bombay: Lalvani Publishers, 1972).

27. Harris, "The Cultural Ecology," p. 55.

28. Planning Commission, *Report on Evaluation of the Rural Electrification Programme.*

29. *U. S. Cattle and Livestock Statistics.*

30. *Ibid.*

31. *Ibid.*

32. Odend'hal, "Energetics of Indian Cattle."

33. Etienne, *Studies.*
34. *Ibid.*
35. Energy Policy Project, *A Time to Choose.*
36. E. P. Gyftopoulos et al., *Potential Fuel Effectiveness in Industry* (Cambridge, Mass.: Ballinger Publishing Company, 1974).
37. Robert H. Williams, Director of Research, Institute for Public Policy Alternatives, Albany, New York, private communication, December 1974.
38. Raj Krishna, "Unemployment in India," *Indian Journal of Agricultural Economics* 28 (January–March 1973): 20.
39. *Ibid.*
40. *Ibid.*
41. M. S. Mudahar, "Dynamic Analysis of Agricultural Revolution in Punjab, India," Cornell University, Ithaca, New York, July 1974.
42. Raj Krishna, "Measurement of the Direct and Indirect Employment Effects of Agricultural Growth with Technical Change," *Externalities in the Transformation of Agriculture* (Ames: Iowa State University, in press).
43. Etienne, *Studies.*
44. *Ibid.*
45. D. Pimentel et al., "Food Production and the Energy Crisis," *Science* (2 November 1973).
46. Ananda Krishnan, Science Attache, Embassy of India, Washington, D.C., private communication, 1974.
47. F. H. King, *Farmers of Forty Centuries* (Emmaus, Pa.: Rodale Press, 1911).
48. C. H. Best and N. B. Taylor, *The Physiological Basis of Medical Practice* (Baltimore, Md.: Williams & Wilkins Company, 1945).
49. King, *Farmers.*
50. H. van der Schalie, "World Health Organization Project, Egypt 10–A Case History of a Schistosomiasis Control Project," in M. Taghi Farvar and J. P. Milton (eds.), *The Careless Technology* (Garden City, N.Y.: The Natural History Press, 1972).
51. Crop Reporting Board of the Statistical Reporting Services, *Agricultural Prices* (Washington, D.C.: U. S. Department of Agriculture, September 1974).
52. A. B. Makhijani and A. J. Lichtenberg, "An Assessment of Energy and Materials Utilization in the U.S.A.," Electronics Research Laboratory Memorandum ERL-310 (revised), University of California, Berkeley, September 1971.
53. Gyftopoulos et al., *Potential Fuel Effectiveness.*
54. C. R. Prasad, K. Krishna Prasad, and A. K. N. Reddy, "Biogas Plants: Prospects, Problems, and Tasks," *Economic and Political Weekly* (Bombay) (August 1974).
55. *Ibid.*

Chapter Four

Fuel for Agriculture

Poor countries need all the energy they can get, as cheaply as they can get it. Previously, development policy in most underdeveloped countries has bypassed the proper management and effective use of "noncommercial" energy sources partly because cheap oil was available, but also because technology is usually borrowed from the industrialized countries which have failed to develop and tap these sources of energy.[1,2]

We wish to examine, in light of the discussion of energy needs, and also in view of the large increases in the prices of oil and fertilizers in 1973 and 1974, the economics of decentralized energy sources in providing fuel and electricity to Third World villages. A comparison of some decentralized systems with current methods of providing energy for agriculture, primarily in the form of oil and electricity, reveals that in many instances the decentralized approaches are less costly while in others the centralized approach is more appropriate. In all instances that we have studied, investments can and should be used more fully so as to reduce the capital costs of development and to increase the opportunities for productive employment.

Among the decentralized technologies, we have devoted the most attention to the conversion of organic materials to gas in village biogas plants because it appears to be an economical way to provide fuel and fertilizers for Third World villages with a great, but so far almost untapped, potential. There is another important reason. The basic raw materials for producing fuel and fertilizer in biogas plants—crop residues—increase as agriculture becomes more productive. In fact, the agriculture sector has the potential of taking care of its own energy needs and having some left over for the rest of the economy as well (being a net supplier of energy to the economy). In each of the prototypical villages of Chapter Two, the potential availability of biogas is larger than the fuels now used for farm machines and irrigation. Even in places where present fuel use is large, as in Arango, Mexico, the potential from biogas is still greater than today's energy use in agriculture. Even in the U.S.A., where the amount of fuel and fertilizers consumed on farms is relatively enormous, potential availability for methane from crop residues and animal dung exceeds energy use for agriculture.[3] Of course, it will take, among other things, time and money to build these energy and fertilizer producing village plants. But the potential is there and will grow with growing agricultural production.

Conventional technologies for providing fuel and electricity for agriculture and industry are not examined here because these have been extensively studied both by governments and by international organizations.

The problems of coal production and use and the potential of hydropower in India, for example, has been the subject of intensive investigation both by the government[4] and the World Bank.[5] The expansion of electric power using large hydroelectric and central station thermal power plants in Southeast Brazil was the subject of an effort that lasted many years.[6]

The economics of these conventional energy sources for supplying energy to industries and villages are relatively well known and well understood. Therefore, we will merely use the experience with conventional energy sources to compare them with some decentralized sources of energy which have not been as intensively studied or tested in practice.

SOLAR ENERGY

The solar energy that falls continually on the earth is the Third World's most abundant energy resource. The solar energy that falls on Saudi Arabia alone *each year* is about equal to the entire proved reserves of coal, oil and natural gas in the world.

The technologies for using solar energy are in varied stages of development. Simple systems which use flat glass collectors to heat water for domestic uses have been commercial for some time and are widely used in Japan. Similar solar heaters which heat air (instead of water) can be used for drying food. Such applications of solar energy are in many cases economical today,[7] but they cannot provide a substantial portion of the energy needed for agriculture.

Technologies to produce mechanical energy or electric power from sunshine are not yet economical. However, the resurgence of interest in solar energy caused by the oil price increases of 1973 and 1974 has already generated a significant amount of progress on various fronts. The direct conversion of solar energy to electricity using solar cells is, for example, being intensively researched, and in the U.S.A. recent reports indicate that a new process may finally reduce the cost of producing silicon solar cells to manageable levels.[8]

An urgent program of research and development of solar energy technologies must be launched by Third World countries, with the cooperation of the oil-exporting nations and the industrialized countries if possible.

Solar energy as manifested in wind may have more immediate application in meeting one of the most pressing energy needs of agriculture: pumping water for irrigation. Producing electricity from wind is expensive, particularly if the electricity must be stored (in batteries, or in a variety of other ways). But windmills for powering pumps may be economically feasible in many areas, especially if the windmills are also used for other purposes, such as sugarcane crushing, when they are not being used to pump water.* An effort to evaluate the economics of windmills for multiple agricultural uses has, to our knowledge, not been made and is urgently needed.

ELECTRIC POWER—INTRODUCTION

The usual way of supplying electric power for rural places is to generate electricity in a large central plant and send it through an extensive transmission network to a wide area. The cost of electricity in the village, from large-scale oil or coal-fired thermal electric generating plants, is the standard against which alternatives are usually measured. It will be the measure here.

Two important values must be carefully established before realistic choices for development can be made. These are the capacity factor and the interest rate for invested capital. "Capacity factor" is the proportion of a power plant's capacity which is actually in use, on the average, over a period of time.

The capacity factor in villages is very low. In India, the average annual rural capacity factor is about 10 percent (800 kwh/kw).[9] This compares with the 40 percent which is characteristic of urban demand in India and many other underdeveloped countries.[10] The effect of such low capacity factors is to greatly amplify the capital cost per unit of electricity generated and to reduce the relative importance of variable costs. Capital-intensive power supply systems will therefore be at a disadvantage unless development takes place simultaneously with electrification and as power becomes available, its use for such purposes as irrigation for multiple cropping rises in such a way as to increase the capacity factor.

The interest rate for capital is an important determining factor in the *choice* of the technology to be used. A commonly accepted rule of thumb is 12 percent[11]; this figure does not include depreciation or inflation. While this interest rate is quite high as compared to rates that are sometimes used to justify

---

*A sufficient reduction in the cost of energy from windmills to make them promising is made possible by the elimination of the electric generators and, particularly, electricity storage. The storage of energy is not critical in this system because the energy requirements are spread over many days. A few windless hours would therefore not affect the system, provided the needed energy is delivered during the several days or weeks when it is needed.

Table 4-1.   Cost of Centralized Electricity Supply (Coal-Fired Generating Plants in India)

Capital cost of central fossil fuel generating station per kw	250	
Transmission cost per kw (20% attributed to rural line)	50	
Rural distribution cost if village is 8 km from line @ $25/km/kw	200	
Total capital cost per kw	500	
Annual interest and depreciation per kw @ 15%	75	
Interest and depreciation per kwhe @ 1,150 kwhe/kw/yr	6.5¢kwhe	—
Interest and depreciation per kwhe @ 800 kwhe/kw/yr	—	9.4¢/kwhe
Approximate fuel and maintenance cost per kwhe	1¢/kwhe	1¢/kwhe
Total Cost	7.5¢/kwhe	10.4¢/kwhe[a]

Notes:

Recent escalations in the price of manufactured goods, copper, and aluminum make it likely that these costs (particularly transmission costs) are lower than the 1974 costs.

The distribution costs assume that about a 100 kw powerline is taken to the village. Higher capacity lines would result in a lower cost/kw and vice versa.

[a]At 16 km from the transmission line the total cost becomes 14¢/kwhe; at 24 km it becomes 18¢ kwhe.

development projects or capital-intensive schemes, we use it to give appropriate weight to the shortage of capital prevalent in most underdeveloped countries.

CENTRALIZED AND DECENTRALIZED (DIESEL) POWER GENERATION

Table 4-1 shows the capital and other costs of generating electricity in central power stations and distributing it to rural places, using coal-fired generating plants. Using India as a concrete example, we discover several critical factors which determine whether centralized or decentralized generation is more economical. These are: the capacity of the distribution system,* the capacity factor, and the distance of the village from a main transmission line.

The cost of electricity delivered to a typical electrified village (that is, a large village) in India is around 8 to 10¢ per kwhe. This is much higher than the 2¢ per kwhe or so actually charged rural customers in India because only the cost of the distribution system is included in calculating what the charge should be. Thus the users of electricity in Indian villages are receiving a continuing large subsidy from the government.

It is almost impossible to generalize accurately about the cost of electricity generated in small diesel sets. Installation and fuel costs will vary from village to village. Nevertheless, in order to clarify our discussion of electrification

---

*The capacity of the distribution system depends on population and the anticipated per capita peak load once the system has been operating a few years.

Table 4-2. Cost of Electricity from Small-Scale Diesel Generator

Capital cost per kw[a]	$250	
Annual depreciation and interest per kw @ 17%[b]	43	
Interest and depreciation @ 1,150 kwhe/kw	3.7¢/kwhe	—
@ 800 kwhe/kw	—	5.3¢/kwhe
Labor, maintenance, etc.[c]	1.3¢/kwhe	1.9¢/kwhe
Fuel cost[d]	6.0¢/kwhe	6.0¢/kwhe
Total cost of electricity	11¢/kwhe	13.2¢/kwhe

[a]Installed high-speed diesel–electric set (100 kw).

[b]Interest at 12 percent depreciation at 5 percent;

[c]Assumes an annual cost of $1500 for a 100 kw plant for labor and maintenance.

[d]Assumes generator efficiency is 25 percent and diesel fuel available in villages at $5.00/million Btu–$3.00/10^6 Btu diesel fuel in major center + 50¢/10^6 Btu distribution mark-up, + $1.50/$10^6$ Btu transportation cost. This last cost assumes a main haul of 500 km at 10¢/ton-km and rough road haul in bullock cart for 20 km at 20¢/ton-km.

alternatives, we will use the costs detailed in Table 4–2. High crude oil prices and the transportation costs in underdeveloped countries make it unlikely that the cost of diesel delivered to the village would be less than $4 or $5 per million Btu. On the whole it appears that electricity from decentralized small-scale diesel generators is more expensive than power from central stations if the village is reasonably large (more than a few hundred people) and less than about 10 km to a high-tension transmission line (see Tables 4–1 and 4–2). As footnote a to Table 4–1 shows, the costs of electricity from central power stations is sensitive to the distance of the village from a high-tension line. Indeed, at $25/kw the local transmission cost quickly becomes the major cost, so that beyond 10 km small-scale diesel plants begin to look attractive. Higher capacity factors, always desirable, would mitigate this effect, and make centralized plants more attractive at longer distances.

In oil-exporting countries, such plants deserve serious consideration as they can be installed quickly. Of course, in countries such as India and Bangladesh, oil competes with food for foreign exchange resources. Other sources of fuel for decentralized plants are more desirable.

USING BIOLOGICAL MATERIALS FOR AN ENERGY SOURCE

Biological materials are the most important immediately viable decentralized energy source for electric power and for mechanical power as well. They can be used directly as fuel or converted to other forms.

The economics and technology of using wood and agricultural wastes directly to raise steam for power production are not very favorable. Capital costs are high and the efficiencies of small plants are low (10 percent).

Steam engine generating plants with a capacity of a few hundred kilowatts cost $600 to $800 per kw. Given the low capacity factors encountered in rural areas, electricity costs of 10¢ to 20¢ per kwhe may be expected even if we ignore fuel costs.

The reduction of capital costs for small- and medium-scale power systems using low grade fuels (those which have a low energy content per ton when compared to bituminous coal), such as wood, peat, and oil shale, should be an important priority for energy research and development because such fuels are widely available. Many are currently economical in large-scale systems. Oil shale, for example, fuels a 1.6 million kilowatt electric generating station in the U.S.S.R. and produces power competitively with central station plants based on coal.[12] The residues from an oil shale power plants can be used for making bricks, as aggregate for concrete, and so on. Many countries have oil shale resources (e.g., Brazil) where this approach may be economically feasible.

The destructive distillation of wood in the absence of air (pyrolysis) is an ancient technology which may be an economic approach to providing fuel for small towns, though not for most villages, since the plants required are too large and the costs of pyrolysis are sensitive to the size of the system.

Pyrolysis of wood (or other organic matter such as newspapers and food wastes) produces charcoal, a medium Btu gas (10,000 to 18,000 Btu per cubic meter compared to about 36,000 Btu for natural gas) and combustible liquids with around 70 percent efficiency.[13,14,15]

We are not aware of any recent attempts to evaluate this old technology—made obsolete by cheap oil—for use in poor countries in view of current high oil prices. However, there are a few indications that the economics of wood pyrolysis may be attractive.

First, wood is currently used in China as a tractor fuel and was used even when prices of oil were low.[16] Possibly the high cost of transporting oil in relatively small quantities to rural areas and the relatively slow pace of China's exploitation of oil resources played a major role in favoring the use of wood in some areas.

Second, wood pyrolysis was phased out in the industrialized countries because of cheap oil and the relatively high cost of labor (associated primarily with the collection and transportation of wood). Neither of these conditions applies today to poor countries.

The capital costs of large plants (1,000 tons per day or more) for pyrolysing municipal wastes in the U.S.A. have been variously estimated to be between $3,000 and $20,000 per ton per day of capacity. These tentative costs are based on "experience with pyrolysing coal and oil and on limited laboratory and pilot plant testing."[17] These costs include some expensive pollution control equipment and are based on the high cost of construction labor in the U.S.A. These two factors would tend to lower capital costs in the poor countries, while the smaller-scale plants needed in most cases would tend to drive them up. If pilot plants built in poor countries show that the capital costs are in the $1,000 to $5,000 per ton per day range, wood pyrolysis could provide a variety of useful and economical fuels, including some substitutes for imported oil, for towns near sources of wood.*

BIOGASIFICATION

Biogasification is perhaps the most important technology for converting biological material to more useful forms of fuel. It can be put to widespread use in the near future, its economics appear favorable, and it produces organic fertilizers in addition to fuel.

In this process complex biological materials are broken down by anaerobic bacteria (that is, bacteria that work in the absence of atmospheric oxygen) to simple organic compounds which are in turn converted to methane and carbon dioxide. Of the biological materials encountered in nature, only mature wood appears to be largely resistant to breakdown. The plant material and manure that comprise most agricultural residues are broken down. (Details and references on the biological, technical and economic aspects of biogasification are given in Appendix B.)

A biogas plant consists of digestors (the receptacles in which the biogasification takes place), facilities for storing and slurrying the residues, and sometimes facilities for grinding the residues and drying the residuum from the digestor. A system large enough to supply a village reliably should include two or three digestors and gas storage.

The digestors produce an intermediate Btu gas (20,000 Btu/cu.m.) consisting primarily of methane (55 to 65 percent by volume) and carbon dioxide. Standard techniques for the removal of carbon dioxide and the small amounts of hydrogen sulfide can purify the gas and produce a high Btu gas (methane) similar to pipeline quality natural gas. The Monfort Company, in Greeley, Colorado (U.S.), plans to build a large biogas plant on its cattle feedlot and sell the purified gas to a natural gas pipeline company.

From the point of view of returning nutrients contained in biological materials to the soil, biogasification has an advantage over ploughing in manure, since the fertilizer is already in usable form, in contrast to manure which must usually be allowed to decompose in the soil for many days before planting. This is especially important with multiple cropping, since prompt planting permits more crops.

The use of biogas as a basic energy resource for villages has been

*At a 70 percent conversion efficiency, one ton per day of (dry) wood would produce about 4 billion Btu of fuel per year. If the plant capacity factor is assumed to be 70 percent, a capacity of one ton per day would yield an annual output of about 3 billion Btu, or about $3,000 if one assumes an overall value of $1 per million Btu for the mix of fuels produced. The annual cost of wood at $5 per ton would be about $1,250.

recommended by the Fuel Policy Committee of India[18] and it is now the object of special study of the National Academy of Sciences of the U.S. as a promising source for supplying energy to villages in the near future. Much of the work on the development of small biogas plants has been done in India,[19,20] and in the past year there has been a resurgence of interest in applying this technology to meet some of India's fuel and fertilizer problems.[21] Thousands of small biogas plants have been built on individual farms, particularly in India and Taiwan. Currently, most of the gas is used for residential purposes.

The basic resource—agricultural residue—is found wherever there are agricultural communities. The technology for converting these residues is also well enough understood for us to make a preliminary economic evaluation and a comparison of the costs of village electrification schemes based on biogas with those based on central station generation.

A possible rather advanced village scheme is outlined in Figure 4–1. (As we shall see, proper phasing and use of capital dictate that such a scheme would be gradually built up over a number of years.) An important feature of this scheme is that farmers are paid for the residues which they deliver. The price paid for the residues will vary from region to region depending largely on the ease of collecting the residue, the suitability of the residue for gasification, and whether the wastes are currently used for other purposes such as cooking. Prices might vary from about 70¢ per million Btu of animal manure in North Indian villages where dried manure is used for cooking fuel and is scarce, to 20¢ per million Btu for crop residues or dung where these are abundant and are not presently used.

Paying for raw fuel on the basis of energy content will favor the delivery of crop residues for they have a much higher energy value per ton than wet manure, which, in its fresh state, has a water content of up to 80 percent. This has an important advantage but may also create a problem which must receive simultaneous attention. The advantage is that it is more efficient to gasify crop residues directly rather than feeding them to animals. If high prices for crop residues deprive cattle of their fodder, the result could be a reduction in the number of cattle (which may or may not be desirable), or still feebler cattle, or more overgrazing of pastures. The price paid for the fuel for the biogas plant should ordinarily be based upon the prevailing wage rate and the fuel and fertilizer value of the material, but it may have to be modified and varied from one year to the next depending on the availability of crop residues to take account of the important indirect effects on the village economy.

The gas the plants produce which is not used immediately for electricity would be compressed and stored. Bottled gas would provide the fuel for farm machines and, *if necessary,* for cooking. The compressed gas could also be taken from storage and used to generate electricity to meet peak demands. Agricultural use of electricity is seasonal, but a digestor can only operate

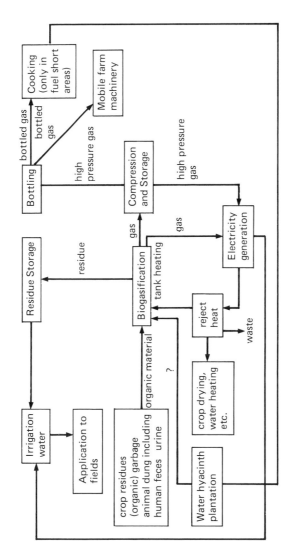

Figure 4–1. Schematic Diagram of Village Biogas-Electricity Scheme System

economically at consistent high capacity factors. Compressed gas storage is relatively inexpensive in both economic and energy terms.

The large amount of waste heat produced in the generating plant (about 75 percent of the total input) would be relatively high grade heat with a temperature of about 300°C. Part of this heat could be used to regulate the digestor temperature. The rest could be used for crop drying, producing raw sugar, heating water for domestic uses, and so on.

The residuum of undigested materials which leaves the digestor is an excellent organic fertilizer. (For many of the high-yielding seed varieties, it will probably be necessary to add chemical fertilizers to the organic sludge in order to have the correct quantity and mix of nutrients that these plants require.) It could be returned to the land either mixed in the irrigation water or as a semi-solid, after dewatering. In some places such as North India and Tanzania, this return of nutrients would mean a large increase from present use of fertilizer. In others, such as China and South India, it would reduce organic fertilizer losses inherent in composting, but the principal benefit from biogasification would be the fuel produced. Digestor residuum does not attract flies which spread many diseases, and digestion at the right temperatures also suppresses the pathogens in human feces.

The safe disposal of human excrement (feces and urine) is one of the most important measures for the prevention of disease in Third World villages.* The pathogens that human excrement harbors (various species of bacteria, protozoa, and helminths) cause a variety of serious diseases such as cholera, typhoid, schistosomiasis, amoebic dysentery, and enteritis. These pathogens can be destroyed by uniform heating to 60°C for 30 minutes to one hour. In anaerobic digestors that operate in the intermediate temperature (mesophilic) range 25°C to 40°C, the pathogens may take several weeks to be destroyed. However, it is not clear whether organisms are as completely destroyed in the mesophilic temperature range as they are in the thermophilic (40° to 60°C) which would apply to properly managed compost piles, or to anaerobic digestors, appropriately heated, for example, with waste heat from a biogas-electricity generating plant. If field data indicate that intermediate temperatures are not effective, and an electric generator is not installed with the biogas plant, then heating the excrement to the requisite temperature with gas before feeding it to the digestor may be necessary. The amount of heat required would be about equal to the amount of gas generated from the feces. In these circumstances there would be no net gain in fuel from processing the human excrement; the gains would be in improved health and in the output of fertilizer. Composting of excrement, which may be cheaper but more difficult to manage, would achieve the same result.

Apart from the significant health benefits, large quantities of

*This discussion is based on the book *Composting* by H. B. Gotaas (note 22).

fertilizers, particularly fixed nitrogen, can be recovered from human excrement (particularly urine which has a high nitrogen content). Building latrines could be a profitable proposition on the basis of the value of the recovered fertilizer. To induce people to use such latrines, the area or the latrines themselves could be equipped with a supply of water for sanitary purposes. If the operation is conducted on a nonprofit basis, an annual payment could be made to each family for using the latrines, even if the other social, human, and economic benefits are not taken into account.

Some approximate calculations for the costs and value of output for such a scheme are shown in Table 4–3. The cost of latrines is based on estimates for Indian villages made by the Khadi Village Industries Commission[23] to which approximate costs of water supply have been added. An important point to note is that the amount of nitrogen collected from human excrement (three-fourths of it coming from urine) is 75 percent of that available in a much larger quantity of animal dung (excluding animal urine).

The labor required to collect the organic materials for the biogas

Table 4–3. Approximate Economics of Installing Latrines in Mangaon for the Recovery of Fertilizers

1. Cost of 20 latrines excluding piping and water supply @ 50 each[a]	$1,000
2. Water supply and piping for 20 latrines	1,000
3. Pump and piping to feed excrement to the biogas plant	1,000
4. Total capital cost	$3,000
5. Annual interest (12%) and depreciation (3%)	$ 450
6. Annual labor cost (1 man-year)	300
7. Total annual operating cost	$ 750
8. Value of nitrogen (80% of potential[b] at $400/ton)	$1,200
9. Value of P_2O_5 (80% of potential[b] at $250/ton)	250
10. Value of K_2O (80% of potential[b] at $150/ton)	100
11. Total value of annual output[c]	$1,550
12. Possible annual incentive payment per family of five	$ 4

[a]One latrine for 10 families (50 people). One well, a small pump, and pipes would be the main costs of the water supply system.

[b]We have assumed the lower end of the values for the normal amount and the nutrient content of the human excrement (including urine) per person. As the people eat more and get more protein, more nitrogen becomes available in the excrement. We have taken credit for all the nitrogen collected even though much or most of the human excrement is deposited in the fields. With current practice, however, the nitrogen excrement is not uniformly spread and is not available to most plants in the field. Some damage may even be caused to plants near the areas where people urinate. While some of the nitrogen would become available to the next crop after ploughing, most of it (which is in the form of water soluble urea) would be lost by leaching, by volatilization, and by bacterial degradation.

[c]The fuel value of the excrement has not been taken into account because it is assumed (conservatively) that the biogas generated from the human excrement will be used to pre-heat the feces to destroy disease-carrying organisms.

plant would not need specialized training. General instruction in proper management of animal wastes, particularly urine, would be sufficient. A trained villager could operate a village biogas plant. More highly trained maintenance and management personnel stationed in market towns serving 10 to 15 villages,* could provide assistance, and could take care of routine troubleshooting in a complete biogas-electricity system. Still more highly specialized services might be provided from a regional center. This linking together of energy development at the village, market town and regional levels, like the integration of other activities at these levels, as discussed earlier in this book and in many excellent works on the subject, is essential to the success of decentralized electrification.

The great problems in village development, including energy development, are political and organizational. Discussion of the merits and problems of decentralized schemes have rarely addressed this question.

Decentralized energy systems have often been dismissed on the grounds that maintenance would be difficult. We mentioned earlier that electricity use in Indian villages declines even when the electricity comes from a centralized source, which points to a lack of maintenance in the villages. Much of the capital investment for agricultural development must be made in the villages, in tubewells, pumps, motors, irrigation channels, and so on, whatever the source of fertilizers or power. If these facilities are not maintained, then no program can achieve the goal of agricultural progress. If the personnel to service these essentially decentralized aspects of agricultural development are available, then the added problems of biogas plants and decentralized electricity generation should not be difficult.

To estimate the energy from wastes available for power generation, we must know the energy content of the basic resource—the agricultural residues. Neither the quantities nor the energy content of crop residues in villages have been satisfactorily measured. Accurate estimates require the following information: (a) a breakdown of crop production in individual villages; (b) the agricultural residues associated with each ton of harvested crop; (c) the amount of crop residues consumed by animals; (d) statistics for the animal population, including both numbers of animals of each type and the average weight of these animals; (e) data relating to manure production and its quality with due regard to feeding conditions normally encountered in villages, and the ease of collection of the manure.

None of this information is available in any authorative form. We have nevertheless attempted preliminary estimates of the available energy residues in the prototype villages described in Chapter Two, which are representative of many agricultural societies in the Third World.

Table 4–4 shows the amount of residues associated with a ton of

*The area that market towns can serve depends on a number of factors including the rapidity of the means of transportation.

Table 4-4. Estimated Residue Coefficients for Major Crops

		Residue Coefficient[a]
Husked rice[b]	early varieties[c]	1.85
	late varieties[c]	2.90
Paddy[b]	early varieties[c]	1.25
	late varieties[c]	1.95
Corn[e]		1.20
Cotton[d]		3.00[f]
Soybean[d]		2.60[g]
Wheat[d]		1.75
Barley[d]		1.50
Rye[d]		1.95
Oats[d]		1.75
Grain sorghum[d]		0.85
Sugar cane[d]		0.25
Potato, cassava[d]		0.20[h]

[a]Residue coefficient is the ratio of the weight of *dry matter* of residue to recorded harvested weight at field moisture. For grains and straw field moisture content is assumed to be 15 percent.

[b]Data are for India and are for the same crops (FAI, 1969).[24] Paddy is unhusked rice, when using agricultural statistics to determine residues. It is important to note whether the statistics are for rice or paddy. In calculating the residues from FAI (1969), rice hulls are included as residue. For early-maturing varieties they amount to about 30 percent of the residue, while for late-maturing varieties they amount to about 20 percent of total residue.

[c]The major distinction in straw to grain ratios is not between dwarf and tall varieties of rice (see FAI, 1969, p. 43) but between early and late maturing varieties, the former including the new high-yielding varieties.

[d]Residue coefficients as determined by individual crop experts and forwarded by Dr. Robert Yeck of the Agricultural Research Service of the United States Department of Agriculture, Washington, D.C.[25] Small grain estimates were for straw and an additional factor of 0.25 for chaff has been included.

[e]There is a wide disparity in estimates of corn residue coefficients. IR&T (1972) estimate 0.55. [26] SRI (1974) use figures that imply a coefficient of 1.2.[27]

[f]Both lint and seed are included in the harvested crop.

[g]Based on SRI (1974) other estimates of residue coefficients are: IR&T (1972) 0.55; and 0.85-2.6 by the USDA as in (d) above. Soybean is taken to be representative of other legumes.

[h]Data for potato comparison made on basis of similarity of habit.

harvested crop. These estimates are crude not only because of the scattered measurements but, more importantly, because crop residues vary with the variety of seed that is used.

Table 4–5 shows the data on the production of dung and its fertilizer value. These data have been used to compute amount of energy and fertilizer available in organic wastes of the protypical villages of Chapter Two. The results are shown in Tables 4–6 and 4–7.

Table 4–6 shows that the amount of per capita energy that could be

Table 4-5. Manure Production Data

Animal	Fresh Manure per 1,000 kg Liveweight (kg/yr)	Assumed Average Liveweight (kg)	Fresh Manure Production Assumed per Head (kg/yr Except Item 7)	Assumed Moisture Content of Fresh Manure (Percent)	Nitrogen Content Percentage of Dry Matter	
					Solid and Liquid Wastes	Solid Wastes Only
1. Cattle	27,000	200	5400	80	2.4	1.2
2. Horses, mules, donkeys	18,000	150	2700	80	1.7	1.1
3. Pigs	30,000	50	1500	80	3.75	1.8
4. Sheep and goats	13,000	40	500	70	4.1	2.0
5. Poultry	9,000	1.5	13	60	6.3	6.3
6. Human feces without urine	—	40 to 80	50 to 100	66 to 80	—	5 to 7
7. Human urine[a]	—	40 to 80	18 to 25 kg dry solids/yr	—	15 to 19 (urine only)	—

Source: Note 22.

[a]We have not used the extreme of variations of nitrogen in human urine discussed in Chapter Three, but rather the more usual range as cited in note 22.

Table 4-6. Energy Supply from Agricultural and Animal Wastes

Village	Population	Crop Residues[a] 10⁶ Btu/yr	Crop Residue Eaten by Animals[b] %	Crop Residue Eaten by Animals[b] 10⁶ Btu/yr	Dung 10⁶ Btu/yr	Net Energy Available from Wastes[c] 10⁶ Btu/yr	Collectable Wastes[d] 10⁶ Btu/yr	Potential Biogas from Wastes[e] 10⁶ Btu/yr	Current Fuel Use for Farm Machines and Irrigation 10⁶ Btu/yr	Potential per Capita Energy from Biogas 10⁶ Btu/yr
1. Mangaon, India	1,000	8,000	70	6,000	6,000	8,000	6,000	3,600	0	3.6
2. Peipan, China	1,000	20,000	30	6,000	5,000	19,000	14,000	8,400	3,000	8.4
3. Kilombero, Tanzania	100	800	10	100	500	1,200	800	500	0	5.0
4. Batagawara, Nigeria	1,400	6,000	10	600	7,000	12,000	9,000	5,400	0	3.9
5. Arango, Mexico	420	30,000	10	3,000	1,300	28,000	22,000	13,000	11,000	31.0
6. Quebrada, Bolivia (one *parcela*)	6	20	10	2	30	50	35	20	0	3.3

[a] This table has been compiled from the data on residues in Tables 4–4 and 4–5 and from the agricultural production data in Chapter Two. Numbers are rounded. The energy value of crop residues is taken as 15 million Btu/ton, and dung at 14 million Btu/ton on a dry basis.

[b] We assume that in India and China, where grazing land is scarce, animals eat a large proportion of the crop residues. In Kilombero, Batagawara, and Quebrada, we assume that sufficient grazing land is available so that the animals get most of their food from the pastures. In Arango, the residues are so large that only a small fraction is required to feed the animals.

[c] Net energy from wastes is equal to the energy value of the dung plus the crop residues not fed to the animals.

[d] We have assumed that a maximum of 70 percent of the cattle and horse dung can be collected, 80 percent for pig dung, and 30 percent for the dung of sheep, goats, and chickens. The efficiency of collection could possibly be even higher if the animals were kept in properly designed sheds. For crop residues, we assume that 80 percent of the residues not fed to animals can be collected.

[e] We assume a biogasification efficiency of 60 percent. This is a simplification because the yield will depend on the temperature in the digestor, its design and the mix of the materials put into it. However, considering the uncertainty in the data, this assumption is probably a relatively minor source of error.

Table 4-7. Annual Organic Nitrogen Supply in the Case Study Villages

Place	Cultivated Land ha	Nitrogen Available in Net Residues[a] kg.	Excluding Human Excrement — Nitrogen in Collectable Wastes[b] (Solid Only) kg.	Excluding Human Excrement — Nitrogen in Collectable Wastes[c] (Solid and Liquid) Included, kg.	Nitrogen Collectable in Human Excrement (Solid and Liquid) kg.[d]	Total Nitrogen Collectable in Solid and Liquid Wastes	Nitrogen Available per Hectare Cultivated Land per Year
Mangaon, India	300	10,000	4,000	7,000	3,000	10,000	33
Peipan, China[e]	200	13,000	7,000	9,000	4,000	13,000	65
Kilombero, Tanzania	60	1,000	500	800	300	1,100	18
Batagawara, Nigeria	530	13,000	6,000	9,000	4,200	13,200	25
Arango, Mexico[e]	380	7,000	5,000	6,000	1,700	7,700	20
Quebrada, Bolivia (one parcela)	1	70	40	50	18	68	68

[a] We have assumed a nitrogen content of 0.2 percent for crop residues.

[b] For animal and human excrement we have used the data shown in Table 4-5.

[c] Net residues calculated as in Table 4-6.

[d] We assume that a maximum of 80 percent of the nitrogen in human excrement can be collected. For Arango and Peipan we have used intermediate values for the total nitrogen excreted per person per year, and for the other villages we have used the low end of the range shown in Table 4-5. The rationale is that people of Arango and Peipan have more adequate diets which are also higher in nitrogen content (protein).

[e] The nitrogen figures for Peipan and Arango are probably underestimates since the crops are currently well fertilized. The nitrogen content of the crop residues is probably considerably higher, especially since corn (which has a high nitrogen content in the residue) is a major crop in both areas.

generated in the form of biogas—which can be used to power irrigation, farm machines, and goods transportation—is not the same in all the villages. Arango, Mexico, contains much the largest potential. *This reminds us that as agricultural production increases, the production of crop residues increases with it. In energy terms, increasing yields of crop means that we capture solar energy more efficiently. Crop residues can provide increasing amounts of energy to support a growing agriculture.*

We also see from Table 4–6 that the energy use for irrigation and farm machines is in each case lower than the potential availability of biogas.

Table 4–7 shows a somewhat different picture for fertilizers. Except in the cases of Arango and Peipan, the quantities are several times the amounts of nitrogen fertilizers that are now used. But the available nitrogen fertilizer from manure varies a good deal and is often not sufficient to allow the use of high-yielding seed varieties. Thus other sources of fertilizer are necessary. Phosphorous, potassium, and other trace minerals must usually be mined. (Ashes left over from wood burning contain a large quantity of potassium, about 5 percent by weight, and smaller quantities of phosphorous, about 0.5 percent, and other nutrients.) Fortunately, these mineral fertilizers are less expensive than chemical nitrogen both because the per unit prices are lower and the amounts needed are usually less than the amount of nitrogen needed. Fixed nitrogen can be produced in a number of ways (Chapter Three). Rotating crops and planting legumes can not only provide protein for humans and animals but also can produce nitrogen for the soil from the crop residues and the enriched human excrement which the crop indirectly produces.

In most cases, however, planting several crops each year will require the use of chemical nitrogen. For example, a crop of soybeans plus all the collectable organic wastes in Mangaon would provide perhaps half of the nitrogen requirements for growing a crop of rice and a crop of wheat in the same year. It would, of course, be a long time before Mangaon could achieve such an advanced stage of agricultural development. We use this calculation only to illustrate that the use of wastes and chemical fertilizers are not mutually exclusive but, rather, complementary.

COST OF A BIOGAS-ELECTRICITY SYSTEM IN MANGAON

In this section we compare the costs of a biogas-electricity system in Mangaon with the costs of conventional rural electrification projects in India which are based on centralized electricity generation.

In comparing the costs of electricity produced in a biogas-electric power system with a centralized system, one should take into account the value of the fertilizer returned from the system to the land. In Mangaon this nutrient value is now lost, as virtually all collected manure is burned as fuel.

Table 4–8. Fertilizer Prices Paid by U.S. Farmers

	Price in $/Ton		
Fertilizer	*September 1974*	*September 1973*	*September 1972*
1. Nitrogen (based on the price of urea with a 46% nitrogen content)	555	231	198
2. Phosphorous (P_2O_5), (based on superphosphate with 46% P_2O_5 content)	451	225	187
3. Potassium (K_2O), (based on potash with 60% K_2O content)	167	117	105

Source: Note 28.

We have assigned a value of $400 per ton of nitrogen content, $250 per ton of phosphorous (P_2O_5) content, and $150 per ton of potassium (K_2O) content. These are lower than the September 1974 prices paid by U.S. farmers shown in Table 4–8. The prices paid by U.S. farmers have historically been considerably lower than those paid by farmers in other countries.[29] The (official) prices paid by Indian farmers for urea in October 1973 were, for example, about $300 per ton of nitrogen content[30] or 30 percent higher than the September 1973 prices paid by U.S. farmers. Since September 1973 the prices of nitrogen in the U.S. have more than doubled. Prasad, Prasad, and Reddy cited a retail price of nitrogen in India of about $550 per ton in June 1974.[31] * Moreover the actual prices paid by Indian farmers who cannot acquire fertilizers directly from the government may be much higher, and a bag of fertilizer may change hands and prices several times before it is applied to the field.[32] We have used lower estimates than prevalent prices in order not to underestimate the costs of operating biogas plants.

Table 4–9 shows the capital costs for two biogas-electricity schemes, one with provisions for supplying gas for cooking, the other without. The cost shown in column A indicates that if half the biogas produced is used for cooking, the capital costs of the biogas is only slightly less than that for a centralized scheme (assuming a main transmission line exists at distance 8 kilometers from Mangaon, Table 4–1, Chapter Four). This arises not only

*The high cost of chemical fertilizers, usually in foreign exchange, points up the great value of composting as an immediate and cheap source of fertilizers in places where agricultural, animal, and human wastes are not now used. Only unskilled labor and some extension workers are needed to implement a composting program. Though composting (aerobic fermentation) does not yield fuel, as biogasification does, it will take time and money to build biogas plants, and composting could serve as a valuable stop-gap measure.

Table 4–9.   Capital Costs of Biogasification-Electrification System in Mangaon (in 1974 Dollars)

	With Cooking Fuel *A*	*Without Cooking Fuel* *B*
Biogasification plant[a]	8,000	8,000
Gas plant auxiliaries	1,000	1,000
Land cost	1,000	1,000
Gas storage and compression[b]	1,500	1,500
Cooking fuel distribution cylinders and gas stoves[e]	8,000	—
Electric generator with reciprocating gas engine and switchgear @ $160/kw installed[d]	12,000	22,500
Construction supervision and training[c]	1,000	1,000
Subtotal	32,500	35,000
Interest on capital during six months' construction @ 12%)	2,000	2,000
Total	34,500	37,000
Cost per kw	$460	$265

[a]See Appendix B. We assume two digestors, each producing 140 cubic meters of biogas per day. The gas production in columns A and B is the same. Exclusive of the energy use in the biogas plant, the digestors will produce about 2 billion Btu of fuel per year. Digestor costs based on notes 19, 20, 21.

[b]Storage for 50 percent annual production of unscrubbed gas.

[c]Includes $6,000 capital cost for market town headquarters for 12 villages.

[d]Based on mid-1974 quotation from a manufacturer in the U.S.A. and includes approximate shipping costs. In the scheme with cooking fuel we have 75 kw generator (Col. 1); without cooking fuel the entire output of the gas plant goes to the 240 kw generator. A gasoline engine or diesel engine can be substituted for the gas engine.

[e]Column A assumes all 200 families in the village use methane for cooking, $6,000 for cylinders, $2,000 for stoves. Column B assumes zero use.

because of the costs of distributing and using cooking fuel but, more importantly, because only half of the gas produced can be used to generate electricity. The capital cost per kilowatt of the biogas-electricity scheme without gas for cooking (column B, Table 4–9) is about half that of the centralized scheme.

To reduce capital costs in the Gangetic plain, where fuel is in short supply and dung and crop residues are used for cooking, it will be essential to provide a cooking fuel cheaper than biogas so that the entire output of gas can be used for productive purposes. The washery byproducts of Bihar's coal mines for example, be used as a cooking fuel.* However, since we do not have estimates of the costs, we will not discuss it further.

One way to reduce the costs of supplying cooking fuel would be to

*The Report of the Energy Survey of India Committee[33] recommended this step in 1965, but did not provide cost estimates.

increase the efficiency of burning crop residues and dung directly so that surplus crop residues and dung can be gasified for use in agriculture. Efficient stoves designed along the lines of wood burning stoves[34] now marketed in the U.S. but made of local materials like clay or bricks might be suitable. The *Magan Choola,* a cooking stove designed for use in Indian villages,[35] modified to include downdraft circulation could also be used. Burning dung and crop residues involves the loss of significant quantities of fertilizers and should be viewed only as a stop-gap measure until alternate fuels become available.

Prasad, Prasad, and Reddy, in their recent investigation of the economics of biogas plants in India,[36] considered the possibility of water hyacinth plantations as a source of raw materials for gasification in biogas plants. The water hyacinth, a very efficient convertor of solar energy producing 125 to 200 tons of dry matter per hectare per year, could also be grown for direct use as cooking fuel in brick or clay stoves, bypassing the gasification step.* A one hectare tank supplying 140 tons of water hyacinths a year (about 2 billion Btu) would provide sufficient cooking fuel for Mangaon, if the fuel is used at twice the efficiency of current use, but half the efficiency of gas burners.

Table 4—10 shows an approximate estimate of the costs of a biogas-electricity system combined with a one hectare water hyacinth plantation for cooking fuel supply. While the capital costs for the provision for cooking fuel with water hyacinths are assumed to be greater than that of distributing and using biogas for cooking ($10,000 compared with $8,000), the cost per kilowatt of the biogas-electricity-water hyacinth scheme is much lower—$335 per kw compared to $460. This is because the entire capacity of the digestors and storage can be devoted to electricity generation when the water hyacinth plantation supplies the cooking fuel, whereas half the capacity of the biogas plant has to be devoted to providing cooking fuel. The opportunity cost of using one hectare of land to supply cooking fuel would be negligible compared to the benefit, since 1 billion Btu of biogas could irrigate two crops a year on 200 hectares of land in Mangaon.

In most villages of the world fuel supplies are not as tight as they are in the Gangetic plain. In fact, in most areas dung is not used as a fuel and there are surplus crop residues which, if collected and gasified, would increase the fuel available for use in agriculture. For villages in such areas it would not be necessary to supply gas for cooking and the capital required for a biogas plant or a biogas-electricity system (per unit of annual gas production or per installed kilowatt) would be less than that for a village of comparable population in the Gangetic plain.

The annual costs of the three schemes (shown in columns A and B of

---

*Experiments with biogasification of water hyacinths (of which we are aware) have not so far yielded good results (Appendix B). Experimental and field data are also necessary to determine the burning characteristics of dewatered and dried water hyacinths in cooking stoves.

Table 4-10. Capital Cost of Biogas-Electric System with Water Hyacinth for Cooking Fuel

1. Biogas-electricity system with cooking fuel[a]	$37,000
2. 1 hectare water hyacinth plantation[b]	2,000
3. 200 cooking stoves at $30 each	6,000
4. Water hyacinth dewatering, storage, and distribution	2,000
5. Total	$47,000
6. Capital cost per kw	$ 335

[a]140 kw generator. Annual biogas production 2 billion Btu. See Table 4-9, column B.

[b]The construction costs of a water hyacinth plantation are assumed to be about the same as those of a fish tank. The costs of the latter have been obtained from the *Musahri Plan* (note 37).

Table 4-9 and in Table 4-10) are shown in Table 4-11. With the conservative assumptions that are used in calculating these costs, the cost of electricity produced in the scheme in which biogas would be is distributed as cooking fuel is slightly higher than the cost of the centralized scheme shown in Table 4-1 of this chapter. For the other two cases the cost of electricity would be considerably lower (5.8¢ per kwhe compared to 7.5¢/kwhe). In the case where water hyacinth is distributed as cooking fuel, the price charged is $1.00 per million Btu, and its efficiency of use is assumed to be half that of the gas stove. It is assumed that no charge will be made for the special stoves needed in either case.

One of the conclusions to be drawn from Tables 4-9 and 4-11 is that, contrary to current practice, biogas should not be used for cooking unless necessary.

The cost of manure collection in Table 4-11 is high because it is assumed that only animal dung is used in the biogas plant. Crop residues contain about five times as much energy per ton as wet dung so that the cost per million Btu of input to the digestor, and hence the cost of electricity, would be lowered as more crop residues are used (that is, as more food is grown and surplus crop residues become available). The cost of electricity depends critically on the fertilizer content of the residuum in the biogas digestors. In Table 4-11 we have assumed that only the nitogen in the solid portion of the dung is available. This gives an annual production of four tons of nitrogen, two tons of phosphorous (P_2O_5), and two tons of potassium (K_2O). Proper preparation of household stables (or common stables) with straw, sawdust, and other cellulose litter will absorb the urine (see note 22). This would increase the nitrogen available to seven tons per year with smaller increases in phosphorous and potassium. The nitrogen can be further increased to 10 tons of nitrogen per year if latrines for collecting human excrement are installed and widely used. The data in Table 4-12 show that when animal urine is included the cost of electricity in all cases

Table 4-11. Annual Costs for Three Biogas-Electricity Schemes for Mangaon, India

	A *With Biogas for Cooking Fuel*	*B* *No Cooking Fuel Provision*	*C* *Water Hyacinth Plantations for Cooking Fuel*
1. Annual interest and and depreciation[a]	$ 5,700	6,100	7,600
2. Residue collection at $2/ton fresh manure	2,600	2,600	2,600
3. Local labor and maintenance[b]	1,300	1,300	1,300
4. Market town services	500	500	500
5. Labor for distributing cooking fuel[c]	300	–	600
6. Gross annual costs	$10,400	10,500	12,600
7. Credit for cooking fuel sales[d]	$ 2,000	–	2,000
8. Credit for fertilizer[e]	2,400	2,400	2,400
9. Total credits	$ 4,400	2,400	4,400
10. Net annual operating cost	$ 6,000	8,100	8,200
11. Annual electricity generation at 1,000 kwhe/hw[f]	75,000 kwhe	140,000 kwhe	140,000 kwhe
12. Cost per kwhe	8.0¢	5.8¢	5.9¢

[a]Interest rate 12 percent. Biogas plant (digestors) and water hyacinth plantation depreciated at 3 percent per year, other capital at 5 percent per year.

[b]About one man-year, plus parts.

[c]One man-year for distributing gas. Two man-years for processing and distributing water hyacinths.

[d]Charge for biogas used for cooking $2.00 per million Btu. Charge for water hyacinth for cooking $1.00 per million Btu. Cooking stoves provided free.

[e]Credit taken only for fertilizers available in the solid portion of collected dung—four tons of nitrogen at $400 per ton, two tons of phosphorous (P_2O_5) at $250 per ton, and two tons of potassium (K_2O) at $150 per ton.

[f]Engine-generator efficiency 25 percent. An electricity generation of 1,000 kwhe/kw has been assumed. This capacity factor is less than capacity factor of 1,150 kwhe/kw used for centralized plants for the purposes of comparing the two systems because the decentralized plants will require a somewhat larger installed capacity for the same load due to relatively heavy demand that motor starting requirements will place on the decentralized system.

is lower than that of the centralized system. The costs of electricity and biogas are lowest when human excrement is also used. The cost of compressed biogas for agricultural use is also shown in Table 4–12.

REDUCING CAPITAL COSTS

The foregoing discussion of costs is based entirely on current patterns of electricity use. These are wasteful of capital. Rapid development will require

Table 4–12. Variation of Biogas and Electricity Cost with Fertilizer Content of Residuum in Three Biogas-Electricity Schemes

| | Cents per kwhe | | | | | |
| | *A*
With Biogas for Cooking Fuel | | *B*
No Cooking Fuel Provision | | *C*
Water Hyacinth Plantation for Cooking Fuel | |
	Electricity ¢/kwhe	*$/million Btu Compressed Biogas for Agricultural Use b*	*Electricity ¢/kwhe*	*$/million Btu Compressed Biogas for Agricultural Use b*	*Electricity ¢/kwhe*	*$/million Btu Compressed Biogas for Agricultural Use b*
1. Fertilizer content of nitrogen in solid portion of animal dung	3.0	3.60	5.8	2.05	5.9	2.10
2. Fertilizer content of solid and liquid animal excrement	6.4	2.40	4.9	1.45	5	1.50
3. Fertilizer content of animal and human excrement (solid & liquid) [a]	5.3	1.60	4.4	1.05	4.4	1.10

Note: Values of fertilizer are the same as those used in Table 4–11.

[a]The electricity costs in row 3 have been calculated after including the added costs of latrines (Table 4–3). Assumed capacity factor is 1,000 kwhe/kw.

[b]Biogas costs have been calculated from Tables 4–9, 4–10, 4–11, with the capital costs of the electricity generating equipment excluded.

that capital be used much more effectively than it has been previously, the more so for countries that are hard pressed to pay for food, fertilizer, and oil imports. In India rural electrification and irrigation account for almost all the government's rural capital investment. If the cost of these programs is to be reduced—so they can be offered to more people—it is imperative to improve the capacity factors as this will make electricity from whatever source, central or local, and from whatever fuel—cheaper. Figure 4–2 which shows a graph of electricity cost versus capacity factor illustrates this principle, and shows the enormous reduction in electricity cost achieved when improvement of only a few percent is made in the prevalent low capacity factors.

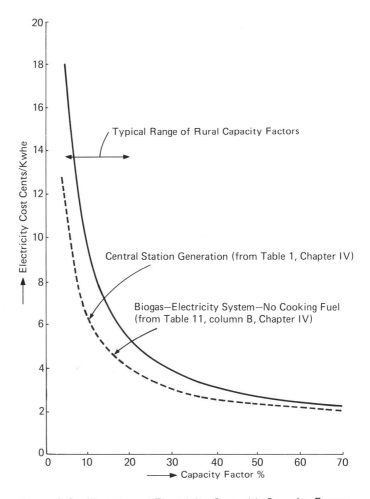

Figure 4-2. Variation of Electricity Cost with Capacity Factor.

In most cases it would be preferable to delay the introduction of electricity until a sufficient capacity for its use has been built up. Irrigation pumps and farm machines could be powered by internal combustion engines (the same ones for both purposes so far as possible). This would reduce the capital cost of providing energy for agriculture considerably. As illustrated in Table 4–13, the costs per unit of useful energy obtained from an internal combustion engine directly are much lower than the corresponding costs for electricity because the intermediate generating step is eliminated. As the small industries in the village develop, electricity could be introduced.

Electricity is desirable for irrigation and for powering stationary small machines because electric motors are more reliable and need much less maintenance than internal combustion engines. After electricity is introduced, the internal combustion engines could be used on farms for transporting surplus produce to market towns as well as for some stationary applications such as sugarcane crushing.

Electrification is important not only for its obvious uses in agriculture but also for the positive psychological effect it has on people's attitudes, for establishing a modest communications system, and so on. From an energy point of view, using local energy resources to generate electricity has an enormous advantage both over centralized generation and the use of fuels in many dispersed internal combustion engines. The waste heat, which is usually 300°C or higher, can be put to many beneficial uses, such as crop drying, raw sugar, manufacture, water heating, operating biogas plants at higher temperatures to produce more gas from the same digestors, district heating in cold areas, combined steam and electricity generation in market towns, and so on.

Figure 4–3 shows a comparison of the efficiency of decentralized systems using agricultural wastes and centralized electricity generating system.

It will be noted that the centralized system can provide electricity only; fuel for machines that power mobile equipment must be provided from another source. Nor can waste heat from the centralized system be delivered economically for agricultural use.

In the three systems using crop residues, little of the waste heat can be recovered if the biogas is compressed and used in dispersed machines. In a system where stationary engines use the gas to generate electricity, large quantities of high-grade usable waste heat are recoverable for the applications mentioned above.

A comparison of two village systems in parts (a) and (b) of Figure 4–3 shows that energy is used more efficiently if crop residues are gasified directly than if the animals are fed these residues and the dung is gasified. The amount of high-grade waste heat to be captured and used is also much greater because the large energy losses of the animals' metabolism are avoided. Of course, animals are the largest source of power on the farm in underdeveloped countries, and this stock of capital should be put to effective use. The amount of useful

Table 4–13.   Comparison of the Costs of Useful Energy for Agricultural Use from Electricity and Biogas (Dollars per Million Btu of Useful Energy)

	A With Biogas for Cooking Fuel		B No Cooking Fuel Provision		C Water Hyacinth Plantation for Cooking	
	Electricity[a]	Biogas[b]	Electricity[a]	Biogas[b]	Electricity[a]	Biogas[b]
1. Fertilizer content in solid portion of animal dung	25.70	18.00	18.80	10.30	19.00	11.00
2. Fertilizer content of solid and liquid animal excrement	20.60	12.00	15.80	7.30	16.00	7.50
3. Fertilizer content of human and animal excrement (solid and liquid)	17.10	8.00	14.20	5.30	14.30	5.50

[a]1 kwhe = 3,413 Btu. Assume efficiency of electricity use = 90%, that is 3,100 Btu of useful energy per kwhe generated.
[b]Assume efficiency of biogas use = 20%, that is 200,000 Btu of useful energy per million Btu of biogas.

Source: Table 13 derived from Table 12 using above efficiencies. Costs rounded to nearest 10 cents. Electricity generating plant capacity factor 1000 kwhe/kw/yr. Higher capacity factors would result in reduced electricity costs.

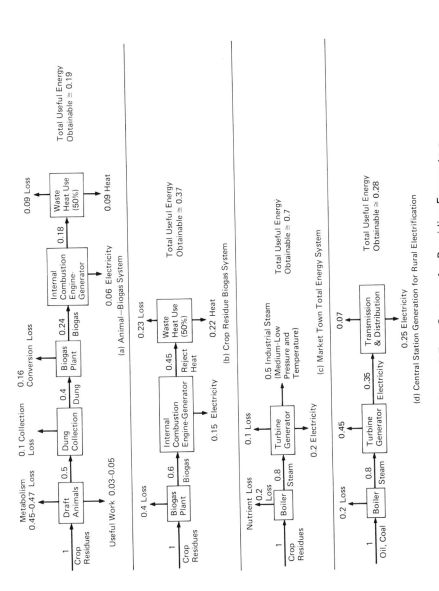

Figure 4-3. Efficiency of Four Systems for Providing Energy to a Village or Market Town

energy derived from draft animals can be increased several fold if the dung is used efficiently. The current efficiency of using crop residues for animal feed, animals for farm work, and dung for cooking is around 6 to 7 percent in India.

Part (c) of Figure 4–3 illustrates a system for using crop residues in market towns to supply electricity and industrial steam.* Such a system is energy efficient, but it has two major disadvantages. First, it fails to recycle most of the nutrients contained in the crop residues; second, for small market towns that do not have a large demand for electricity the system would involve rather high capital cost ($500 to $800 per kw). The total costs could, however, be reduced if the steam were used in an industry with a low capital/output ratio.

Of course, using central power plants to supply electricity to market towns, with populations of 5,000 or more people and diversified industry and commerce, would in many countries be at least as economical as supplying energy with crop residues.** Fuel supply in towns and cities with sewage systems can be increased by the recovery of fuel in sewage treatment plants—a standard technology that operates on the same principle as small biogas plants. In India all large villages and small towns already have electricity. The chief problem is to use the invested capital efficiently, rather than to develop the electricity supply.

But in many African countries, in mountainous regions and other areas where electricity grids do not exist, it would be extremely expensive to create these grids just to supply electricity to market towns and villages. In such cases the question is not whether decentralized or centralized electricity supply is cheaper, but whether electricity can be supplied at all with centralized sources.

The direct employment effects of investing in central power plants versus decentralized village systems are radically different. Leaving aside the increased employment in agriculture that both systems produce, let us focus on the jobs they create directly. Using Mangaon as a model, the village biogas-electricity system creates 10 times more jobs, for the same output, than centralized electricity and fertilizer plants. The number of people required to operate a decentralized system can suit the need for jobs in the village. For example, the number of jobs can be kept constant as energy production expands if some cattle are housed in common sheds, or if more crop residues are used directly for gasification, so that less labor is needed to collect raw material for the biogas plant. Likewise, the plant can gradually be mechanized, if the village's need for jobs levels off.

---

*Dung would probably be too expensive to transport.
**In large market towns, crop residues could be gasified and the gas used as feedstock to manufacture chemical nitrogen. This could only be done when a considerable surplus of crop residues is available. A plant producing 10,000 tons of nitrogen per year would need about 100,000 tons of crop residues per year. This would mean an agricultural area of 1,000 square kilometers (radius about 18 km) would have to generate a crop residue surplus of one ton per hectare to supply the plant.

Finally we compare the overall capital costs of supplying electricity and fertilizers to an Indian village such as Mangaon, India, with the centralized and decentralized schemes. Table 4–14 shows that if biogas is used for cooking, the costs would be only about 15 percent lower than that of the centralized scheme. Using the water hyacinth scheme to supply the cooking fuel would make this decentralized scheme 35 percent cheaper, and if cooking fuel is not required but other conditions are similar to those prevailing in Mangaon, the decentralized scheme costs only half as much as the centralized approach.

Table 4–14. Comparison of Capital Costs for Centralized and Decentralized Schemes, Mangaon, India (Dollars)

| | *Decentralized Schemes* | | | |
| | *A Biogas for Cooking* | *B No Cooking Fuel Provision* | *C Water Hyacinth for Cooking* | *Centralized Scheme* |
Installed Capacity				
75 kw electricity[a] + 4 tons nitrogen per year + 2 tons P_2O_5 per year + 2 tons K_2O per year	34,500	b	b	40,000[c]
75 kw electricity[a] +10 tons nitrogen per year + 3 tons P_2O_5 per year + 3 tons K_2O per year	37,500	b	b	44,000
140 kw electricity + 4 tons nitrogen per year + 2 tons P_2O_5 per year + 2 tons K_2O per year	a	37,000	47,000	73,000
140 kw electricity +10 tons nitrogen per year + 3 tons P_2O_5 per year + 3 tons K_2O per year	a	40,000	50,000	80,000

[a]The higher of the two estimates of fertilizer production in the decentralized scheme include the fertilizer content of animal urine and human excrement (solid and liquid). While the lower estimates include only the fertilizer content of solid animal manure. An approximate capital cost of $3,000 has been added to account for the cost of the latrines (Table 4–3).

[b]The capacity of the digestor is the same in all cases. When biogas is used for cooking, the installed capacity of the electricity system is lower, assuming the same capacity factor.

[c]Centralized electricity supply costs $500 per kw (Table 4–1). The capital cost of a capacity of one ton per nitrogen fertilizer (nitrogen content) per year is about $400 based on the costs of a coal- and oil-based plant currently being built in India. (Capital costs for a natural gas-based plant are around $250 per ton) (note 38). The capital cost of one ton per year of P_2O_5 or K_2) capacity is assumed to be $100.[39] In addition, an investment about $200 per ton per year of nitrogen fertilizer capacity is needed to produce the requisite coal and oil for the fertilizer plant.

FUEL FOR FARM MACHINES

Even more than with rural electrification, a principal problem with supplying fuel for farm machines is not so much the price of oil relative to other sources but the foreign exchange shortage. In many countries, due in part to high oil, fertilizer, and food prices, a lack of enough foreign exchange makes it impossible to import enough oil to fuel farm machines and the irrigation pumps powered by internal combustion engines. Thus in Punjab, Northwest India, which supplies the country with most of its surplus wheat,[40] many tractors and irrigation pumps lay idle in 1974 because farmers could not get enough oil.

In relatively large villages (say, 500 or more people) where gas for cooking is not required, biogas would be a cheaper fuel than oil for fueling farm machines and small trucks or tractors with trailers. For example, a farm machine used 10 hours a day for 15 days will require about 10 million Btu of fuel, assuming an average power output of 5 horsepower. Diesel fuel delivered to the village will cost over 50¢ a gallon (about $4 per million Btu), and gasoline will be even more. Oil costs for such an operation are likely to be about $40, and in all cases this is in foreign exchange funds, either spent or not earned. Fuel from a biogas plant can be provided for $25 or less, including the cost of the gas containers and compression equipment.

Where biogas must be used for cooking *and* no use is made of the fertilizer content of animal urine or human excrement, the costs of biogas and oil for farm machines are comparable.

In villages smaller than 100 people, the costs of the compressors and other equipment needed to bottle this gas may make oil the cheaper alternative even at present high prices, particularly if there are only a few farm machines. The relative economics in such cases would also be greatly affected by the location of the village since transporting oil to remote places is quite expensive. Maintaining equipment properly in isolated places may also be expensive. But if there are many small villages within a radius 10 or 20 kilometers, biogas would probably be the cheaper alternative since common maintenance facilities could be provided. The decision for small villages must be made on a case-by-case basis, considering the development needs and settlement patterns of each area.

In sum, the discussion of energy needs and the calculations presented here indicate that the fuel and fertilizer needs of villages and market towns in the Third World can best be met by a combination of the centralized and decentralized approaches, rather than by the centralized approach alone as has been the case so far. The potential of rural sources of fuel and fertilizers in spurring agricultural growth seems great. Pilot projects are needed to determine more accurately the costs and problems of implementing such decentralized projects in different areas of the Third World.

A SIMPLE ILLUSTRATION RELATING ENERGY
NEEDS AND ENERGY SUPPLY TO
AGRICULTURAL PRODUCTION

As a specific illustration of the concepts presented in Chapters Three and Four, we examine the potential for agricultural development in Mangaon, India. Because of its poverty, and the scarcity and low productivity of land in that region, the resource constraints are greater than they would be in most other regions. In the Sahel region, the problems may be related to long-term climatic changes; in the Andean region it is the scattered nature of the agricultural settlements that presents major social and economic obstacles to development.

A sketch of Mangaon as it is today—with its one crop per year, less than one ton per hectare economy—was presented in Chapter Two. The potential for agricultural production, labor and land productivity, and number of productive jobs, is immensely greater. Water resources are abundant; the land is fertile; there are plenty of fish in the rivers.

To explore the potential of the region, let us examine whether in theory (that is, institutional constraints aside) it is possible for Mangaon to grow enough food for its own people and export half of the food it produces. Let us define "enough food," for simplicity, as 2,500 kilocalories and 70 grams of protein per person per day (see Table 4–15).

We assume that the population of Mangaon will grow at about 2 percent per year. Initially, the provision of medical care will probably increase the population growth rate. However, simultaneous economic development, with due attention to the various factors affecting birth rates, should work toward lowering the birth rate substantially as the development programs take root.

The results of our calculations should not be interpreted literally, for

Table 4–15. Food Needs of Mangaon

1. Gross supply of milled wheat and rice	700 gms/day/person
2. Net supply of wheat and rice assuming 20% for seed and grinding and storage losses.	550 gms/day/person
3. Total annual wheat and rice production requirements for 1,100 people.	290 tons per year
4. Protein intake from grain assuming 7% protein contained in processed grain.	38 gms/day/person
5. Gross protein supply required from other sources (pulses, fish, milk).[a]	35 gms/day/person
6. Total annual protein required from other sources for 1,100 people.	14 tons per year

[a]Pulses, fish, and milk would also provide for the remaining caloric intake.

they are simplified and represent only one hypothetical example of what could be achieved within today's technical and economic constraints.

The principal constraints we consider, other than the fixed amount of agricultural land, are these:

1. No source of energy is available from outside the village. This is related to the foreign exchange shortage which limits oil imports, and to many diverse problems with India's coal industry.

2. No more than 15 kg/ha of chemical nitrogen per year is available during the intial period of five years. This corresponds approximately to India's current capacity to produce chemical nitrogen.*

3. The capital available for borrowing from outside the village is no more than $10 per year per person.

Because of the warm climate, fertile soil, and plentiful supply of water, three or more crops a year can be grown in Mangaon (except sugarcane, which takes a full year to mature). Recall that in the Hunan region of China, which is somewhat colder than Mangaon, growing three crops a year is commonplace.

Growing three crops a year requires irrigation and fertilizers, and we assume it requires one horsepower per hectare of farm machines. Constraints on capital available from outside the village will limit the initial rate at which projects can be undertaken, assuming that, to begin with, there is no capital available in the village.

We assume that a loan of $10,000 per year ($10 per person) can be obtained at a 12 percent interest rate, to be paid back in husked grain at 30¢/kg and that the first payment would be in the fifth or sixth year. Repayment of the principal and interest in the form of food effectively makes the investment inflation-proof, in an economy where prices are in large measure determined by food prices. It would also make it easier to pay for the labor invested in future development projects with food, a policy which is desirable to elicit an adequate supply of labor and good quality of work.

The cost of tubewell irrigation (excluding the cost of the engines and energy supply) is about $150 per hectare.** Farm machines would cost about $20 per hectare ($300 for a 15 horsepower tractor, manual starter). We assume that the engine of the farm machine would also provide the motive power for the irrigation system. If we add $20 per hectare primarily for drainage works (important in the Gangetic plain) and $10 per hectare for contingencies and other small but important investments such as food storage, we find that, excluding energy supply, $10,000 would irrigate and supply the farm machine requirements for about 50 hectares.

---

*Constraints on other fertilizer materials and pesticides are ignored for the sake of simplicity. Organic insecticides, such as the general purpose insecticide extracted from pyrethrum flowers, can be used if necessary.

**Throughout this illustration we have used the data of the *Musahri Plan* written by Ranjit Gupta (note 37) as the basis for estimating the capital costs and employment.

A biogas plant to convert dung to methane and organic fertilizer with a capacity of 1 billion (10^9) Btu of biogas per year would cost about $10,000. This includes interest during construction and facilities for supplying and distributing cooking fuel. Forty percent of the fuel would be set aside for cooking to replace the dung so used.* We have used the estimates for the biogas plant with gas for cooking (column A, Table 4–9, Chapter Four), since the cost for the water hyacinth system (Table 4–10) is somewhat speculative. No electricity would be generated in the initial period, and the gas would supply fuel for cooking (400 million Btu), for farm machines and irrigation pumps on 50 hectares (500–550 million Btu), and for operating the biogas plant compressor and pumps (about 50 million Btu).

The biogas plant would also supply 3 tons of fixed nitrogen, 1 ton of phosphorous (P_2O_5), and 1 ton of potassium (K_2O) per year. We assume conservatively that only one-third of the animal urine is collected with the dung, and that no provision is made to collect human excrement. If 10 kg of chemical nitrogen were available for each of the 300 hectares in Mangaon (that is, about equal to the current use), and if it were used only on the irrigated land, the total supply of nitrogen, organic plus chemical, would be about 120 kg/ha. The phasing of the project should be such that the gas plant is completed before the first tube-well comes on line. The total cost of this initial phase would be $21,000, or about two years' supply of capital. This would include $1,000 for the chemical nitrogen and the $20,000 in capital assets built during the period. Some of the benefits could, however, be derived during the first and second years, since the gas plant can be built in a few months. The construction during this phase would employ about 40 people full time (270 days a year) for two years.

Let us assume that on the 50 irrigated hectares three crops—say, wheat, rice, and green beans—are planted during the third year. A rice yield of 2,000 kg/ha (husked)—which is the average for Punjab, and much less than the yields in Taiwan and Japan—would increase Mangaon's rice supply by 50 percent from 120 tons to about 180 tons; this assumes that the 50 hectares irrigated were initially used for rice production. A wheat yield of 1,500 kg/ha, which is half that often obtained in Punjab with high-yielding varieties, would increase the wheat supply by 300 percent from 25 tons to 100 tons. When this is combined with a bean yield of 1,000 kg/ha (dry weight), the total food production would just about supply Mangaon's food needs as listed in Table 4–15. In addition, the fuel value of the crop residues would be increased from 8×10^9 Btu to about 13×10^9 Btu. Just the extra fuel could supply all of Mangaon's agricultural energy needs for growing three crops a year on each of

---

*Table 2–4, Chapter Two, shows that 2 billion Btu of dung supplies about half the cooking fuel for Mangaon. Producing 1 billion Btu of biogas per year would require about 1.65 billion Btu of dung. This means that 40 percent of the people in Mangaon would need a replacement fuel for cooking.

the 300 hectares. This initial phase would create at least 20 permanent jobs in agriculture and maybe even twice that number.

If the next two years' capital were used in the same fashion, Mangaon could export about 130 tons of grain (wheat and rice) and 50 tons of beans. At 30¢/kg this amounts to $54,000. The total increase in *annual* food production at the end of the fifth year would be about 360 tons—around $108,000. This is about twice the capital invested, including a 12 percent interest rate. From this point on it should theoretically be possible not only to repay the loan but to finance additional development with locally generated savings. Table 4–16 and Figure 4–4 show these financial and production aspects of the scheme in more detail. Note that if 25 percent of the production is retained by the village cooperative to pay back the loan and invest in further development, capital from outside the village is required for only four years.

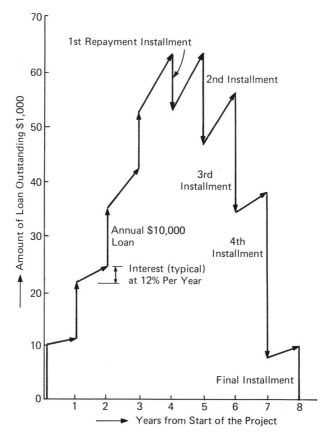

Figure 4–4. Borrowing and Repayment Schedule for Mangaon

Table 4-16.   Investment and Output in a Multiple Cropping Scheme for Mangaon

Year[a]	Annual Loan[b] $	Total Increase in Annual Output[c] $	Locally Generated Annual Savings[d] $	Loan Repayment[e] $	Investment From Local Funds $
0	10,000	—	—	—	—
1	10,000	small	—	—	—
2	10,000	?	—	—	?
3	10,000	54,000	13,000	—	Food Storage[f]
4	—	81,000	20,000	10,000	10,000
5	—	108,000	27,000	17,000	10,000
6	—	135,000	34,000	24,000	10,000
7	—	162,000	40,000	30,000	10,000
8	—	189,000	47,000	9,000	38,000

[a]The number in the column designated "Year" denotes the number of years from the start of the project. For simplicity it is assumed that the entire capital investment is made at the beginning of the year.

[b]The total investment required per hectare is about $200. The annual loan is the capital borrowed from sources outside the village, initially assumed to be the only available development capital.

[c]It is assumed that three crops a year are grown—rice, wheat, and beans—and that the yields per hectare are 2,000 kg and 1,000 kg, respectively. The value of the produce is taken as 30¢/kg. Base yield, i.e., yield before project implementation, is taken as 850 kg/ha.

[d]It is assumed that 25 percent of all the increases in production over the initial production is retained by the village cooperative for loan repayment and further capital investment.

[e]Interest is calculated at 12 percent per year on the unpaid balance.

[f]It is assumed that the savings in year 3 are used to build up emergency food stocks either within the village or in a nearby market town.

According to the Musahri Plan, a plan prepared for the Musahri development block of Bihar by Ranjit Gupta and others[37], the potential for pisciculture in the area is great. A four hectare fishery, including land for the embankments, and so on, would cost about $8,000 and produce about 6,000 kg of fish per year. The annual operating costs are estimated to be about $2,000, including a 12 percent interest on capital. This is probably one of the most rewarding development investments that could be made in the area, for even if one assumes the value of fish to be only $1/kg, the annual output from each hectare would be about $1,500.

Vegetable farming is another area of great promise. It requires the input of much more labor than grains, but the value of the annual output as well as the net profit per unit of land is also much greater.[41]

This illustration is, of course, very simplified. The pattern of investments would change as development proceeds. The investments made in electricity generation, roads, food storage, domestic water supply, fisheries, animal husbandry, marketing surplus food, and so on, would increase while investments in cooking fuel distribution and irrigation pumps would decrease.

As their food needs are fulfilled, people would spend larger and larger portions of their increased income on other essential goods such as better housing or bicycles. This would create additional economic growth and provide for more employment. We have stressed that capital equipment be used as fully as possible so as to decrease the investments needed for small-scale industries. Raj Krishna estimates that the rate of economic growth induced in the nonagricultural sector would be about equal to the growth in agriculture.[42] However, he considers much lower rates of agricultural growth and different mechanization policies than the ones we have discussed in Chapter Three, so that it is difficult for us to judge whether the results of his model apply here.

Relatively small but essential investments for medical care, in afforestation and land conservation, in training people to run and maintain the facilities, and in the organization and administration of the development would be needed. Some areas may require major investments in flood control. Accomplishment of this kind is not possible with the present compartmentalized way of doing things, for it requires careful phasing.

Achieving such progress is not likely to be as fast as we have depicted. But the calculations illustrate that the potential is there for the people of the Gangetic plain to participate fully and fruitfully in economic development, and that this potential can be realized within the rather stringent constraints on capital that exist in India. Growth rates in food production of 15 to 20 percent a year are attainable and were, in fact, achieved in Punjab in the 1966–1970 period.

The resource constraints on development in different countries and regions will, of course, be different. Large biogas plants can hardly be built in the Andean region if the farms remain as scattered as they are; or in the Sahel region if the nomads stay nomads. In some countries, such as Tanzania, land is more plentiful, as is fuel supply, but providing the trained people to initiate rapid agricultural development may be the limiting factor in the short run.

Notes to Chapter Four

1. Energy Policy Project, *A Time to Choose: America's Energy Future* (Cambridge, Mass.: Ballinger Publishing Company, 1974).
2. Alan Poole, "The Potential for Energy Recovery from Organic Wastes," in Robert H. Williams (ed.), *The Energy Conservation Papers* (Cambridge, Mass.: Ballinger Publishing Company, 1975).
3. *Ibid.*
4. *Report of the Energy Survey of India Committee* (New Dehli: Government of India, 1965).
5. *Economic Situation and Prospects of India–Vol. II: The Energy Sector* (Washington, D.C.: International Bank for Reconstruction and Development, 1974).
6. *Power Study of South Central Brazil* (Nassau, Bahamas: Canambra Engineering Consultants Limited, 1966).
7. H. Tabor, "Solar Energy Utilization," Paper presented at the Interregional Seminar on Rural Electrification (of the United Nations), New Dehli, August 1971.
8. Robert Morey Associates (Dana Point, Californi), *Energy Information* 9 (June 1974); 2.
9. Planning Commission, *Report of Evaluation of the Rural Electrification Programme* (New Dehli: Government of India, 1965).
10. *World Energy Supplies 1960–1970,* Statistical Papers, Series J, No. 15, United Nations, New York, 1971.
11. J. Price Gittinger, *Economic Analysis of Agricultural Projects* (Baltimore, Md.: Johns Hopkins Press, 1972).
12. *Oil Shale Utilization: Progress and Prospects* (New York: United Nations, 1967).
13. Judith E. Liebeskind, "Pyrolysis for Solid Waste Management," *Chemtech* (September 1973): 537–542.
14. E. R. Kaiser and S. B. Friedman, "The Pyrolysis of Refuse Components," *Combustion* (May 1968).
15. Bureau of Mines, *Converting Organic Wastes to Oil* (Washington, D.C.: U. S. Department of the Interior, 1971).
16. S. D. Richardson, *Forestry in Communist China* (Baltimore, Md.: Johns Hopkins Press, 1966).
17. Liebeskind, "Pyrolysis."
18. *Report of the Energy Survey of India Committee.*
19. Khadi Village Industries Commission, "Gobar Gas: Why and How," Bombay, India, n.d.

20. Ram Bux Singh, *Biogas Plants* (Ajitmal, Etawah, Uttar Pradesh: Gobar Gas Institute, 1971).
21. C. R. Prasad, K. Krishna Prasad, and A. K. N. Reddy, "Biogas Plants: Prospects, Problems, and Tasks," *Economic and Political Weekly* (Bombay) (August 1974).
22. Harold B. Gotaas, *Composting* (Geneva: World Health Organization, 1956).
23. Khadi Village Industries Commission, "Gobar Gas."
24. V. K. Saolapurkar and S. V. Balkundi, *Rice* (New Dehli: Fertilizer Association of India, 1969).
25. Robert Yeck, Agricultural Research Service, U.S. Department of Agriculture, Washington, D.C., personal communication, 1974.
26. International Research an Technology Corporation, *Problems and Opportunities in the Management of Combustible Solid Wastes* (Washington, D.C.: U. S. Environmental Protection Agency, 1972).
27. Stanford Research Institute, *Effective Utilization of Solar Energy to Produce Clean Fuel* (Washington, D.C.: National Science Foundation, 1974).
28. Crop Reporting Board of the Statistical Reporting Services, *Agricultural Prices* (Washington, D.C.: U. S. Department of Agriculture, 1974).
29. *Production Yearbook 1972,* Vol. 26 (Rome: Food and Agriculture Organization of the United Nations, 1973).
30. *Fertilizer Statistics 1972–1973* (New Dehli: Fertilizer Association of India, December 1973).
31. Prasad, Prasad, and Reddy, "Biogas Plants."
32. Raj Krishna, Senior Economist, World Bank, personal communication, December 1974.
33. *Report of the Energy Survey of India Committee.*
34. Carol H. Stoner (ed.), *Make Your Own Power* (Emmaus, Pa.: Rodale Press, 1974).
35. *Village Technology Handbook* (Mt. Rainier, Md.: Volunteers in Technical Assistance, Inc., 1973).
36. Prasad, Prasad, and Reddy, "Biogas Plants."
37. Ranjit Gupta, *The Musahri Plan* (Patna, India: Association of Voluntary Agencies for Rural Development, 1972).
38. C. J. Pratt, Industrial Projects Division, World Bank, Washington, D.C., private communication, 1973.
39. *Ibid.*
40. M. S. Mudahar, "Dynamic Analysis of Agricultural Revolution in Punjab, India," Cornell University, Ithaca, New York, July 1974.
41. *Ibid.*
42. Raj Krishna, "Measurement of the Direct and Indirect Employment Effects of Agricultural Growth with Technical Change," In *Externalities in the Transformation of Agriculture* (Ames: Iowa State University, in press).

Chapter Five

Energy and Development Policy

Underdeveloped countries can do a great deal more than they are doing to ameliorate the misery of the poor even with the severe burden of limited capital, strained by worldwide increases in food, oil, and fertilizer prices.

Decentralized fuel and fertilizer projects have been stressed in this book because they have been relatively neglected in development strategy whereas they could assume a much larger role. These projects are not a replacement, however, but a supplement to the more conventional energy sources, which must also be exploited. The hydropower resources of Brazil, the coal resources of India, the natural gas of Bangladesh all have a role to play in spurring agricultural growth, and in building the industries and services that are essential to agricultural progress.

These investments in energy supply must be made in accordance with an evaluation of a country's energy needs. In countries where the basic needs of people for food, housing, clothing, water supply, medical care, and the like have been met, there can be considerable debate over the definition of needs. For poor countries the needs are clear. Investments of energy, and of capital and human labor, must be made in those areas which are related to the fulfillment of these basic human needs.

In agriculture the heaviest investments of both energy and capital must go for irrigation works and fertilizers. Farm machines and improving the quality of draft animals that work the fields must also receive high priority in many areas. Corresponding investments should be made in industry to produce the steel, cement, pumps, and so on to supply agriculture with the capital goods it needs to get moving.

Domestic energy needs for cooking and for keeping warm must also be met. Forest and woodland resources must be managed much more carefully if they are not to wither away as they have in many parts of the world. In fuel-short areas, particularly the Gangetic plain, supplying the fuel needed for both domestic and agricultural uses will strain the available capital resources. Nevertheless, as we have shown, it is essential to take care of pressing everyday human needs while at the same time improving fuel management and techniques of burning wood and other vegetable matter. Poor people will meet today's needs as they must, even at the cost of long-run threats to their existence, and development policy must take account of this conflict.

The population problem is another most important instance of the conflict between present needs and long-run development. The enormous demand for peak labor in subsistence agriculture appears to be one of the main reasons for the poor, who cannot afford machines or hired labor, to have many children. Among the other major reasons are lack of medical care, high infant mortality, and the strong imperative many poor rural people feel to have a surviving son. If a couple in an Indian village wishes to be about 95 percent certain that one son will survive to look after them and to tend the fields when they are unable to do so, they must have six children.[1] Three or four of these usually survive to adulthood. For old age, if it comes, most rural families of the Third World can hardly do better than plan for one son to survive.

A successful birth control policy aimed at reducing population growth, desperately needed in most countries, must   concern itself with these peak-labor and medical care aspects of the problem. Provision of medical care and selective mechanization of peak labor operations in agriculture will be essential features.

While steps are being taken to reduce peak labor requirements, simultaneous provision must be made to ensure that the laborers who are displaced have other opportunities for productive employment. Creating opportunities through multiple cropping, vegetable farming, pisciculture, public works, market town development, and so on is important to increase the pace of economic growth and to distribute its benefits equitably. As Mahatma Gandhi so aptly put it in 1934:

> Mechanization is good when hands are too few for the work intended to be accomplished. It is an evil where there are more hands than required for the work as is the case in India. The problem with us is not to find leisure for teeming millions inhabiting our country. The problem is how to utilize their idle-hours which are equal to the working days of six months in the year. Dead machinery must not be pitted against the millions of living machines represented by the villagers scattered in the seven hundred thousand villages of India. Machinery to be well-used has to help and ease human effort.[2]

Creating jobs is not always enough. The proper conditions for work must also be present. In Gambia, for example, the idle season is very important in increasing body weight, which is then expended in the peak season. Under these circumstances, paying people in food to work on public works projects in the slack season would be one way to reduce unemployment during this period, and at the same time improve people's ability to work the fields during the peak periods. Two further examples will illustrate the point.

A friend of the author was involved with a volunteer school building effort in villages in Uttar Pradesh, India. He said that villagers would sit and watch, but would not join in the work that was being done for them. Often they did not think of the school building as a place to hold classes, but a convenient spot for wedding ceremonies and the like. In regard to the last point, many villagers, particularly the older ones, do not think much of education because the schooling system in India, much influenced by the system of the colonial days, creates in young people an antipathy to manual labor and farm work. Since they often cannot find employment outside agriculture, the educated are often not an asset but rather an economic and social burden upon their parents. "Unwillingness" to work and apathy of the poor toward what appears to be in their own interest is directly related to periodic or chronic malnutrition. Why should the villager who subsists on one meal a day put forth an effort to build a building, the benefits of which are far off and marginal, at best?

In contrast, an American missionary armed with wheat wanted to initiate some development in the hill areas of Orissa, among the poorest regions of India. When he started out 10 years ago, he asked the people of the village where the program was to begin what the needs of the village were. The villagers wanted an irrigation tank, but claimed that the 700 people required for two or three months to build the project would not be available. The village could contribute, at most, a tenth of that number. The missionary advised the elders of the village to inquire in the neighboring villages whether the people would work if a day's wages were 1.4 kg. (3 lbs.) of wheat and a few grams of cooking oil.* He said he would be back in a week to see whether the construction of the needed earthen dam could be initiated. The following week 700 workers were on hand and the project was completed on time. This experience was repeated dozens of times during the 10 years he spent working in Orissa.

The portion of the investment in development projects that is payment to workers can, and in food-short areas, should be in the form of food. Four hundred thousand tons of wheat can provide full-time employment (270 working days per man-year) for one million people for one year. At 1974 world prices of wheat, this would cost about $80 million per year.

If such investments are used to create productive assets such as irrigation tanks or wells, they could help to ensure adequate food production in the future while easing current and future employment problems. As an example, an investment in minor irrigation works in India of $2 billion dollars over 5 years, $240 million of which could be in food to pay labor (equivalent of 3 million man-years of labor paid 1.2 million tons of wheat), would create

---

*At 1974 world prices of wheat, this is equivalent to a wage of about 30 cents a day. At the prices of the mid 1960s, it was equivalent to about 10 cents a day.

roughly 3 million permanent jobs in agriculture and increase *annual* food production by approximately 5 million tons (see Chapter Three for details).

Simultaneous investments in roads, fertilizers, and so on could increase food production further, considering the synergistic effects that irrigation, fertilizers, transport and storage of food exert on the availability of food for people.

Development plans are often thrown into disarray because during times of natural disasters, such as droughts, governments must devote large amounts of money to buy food for the hungry. During such catastrophic times governments often delay action until they are virtually forced to it; the problem can no longer be ignored when millions of people begin streaming into the cities in search of food, as they did in the Sahel region, in Bangladesh and in India in 1973 and 1974. By permitting such delays, and often even denying the very existence of serious food shortages, many underdeveloped countries lose their best chance of dealing with the problem. The food which might have been used, with foresight and planning, to create productive assets in the countryside must in the end be given to the hungry anyway—with no long-term benefits to show for it.

Our discussion here has inevitably departed from strict concern with energy and entered into some wider considerations about development. Energy policy is, of course, just one of the strands in development policy and cannot succeed by itself. Equitable, productive distribution of food is fundamental. Not only is it necessary from a practical and a humanitarian point of view; it is also a precondition for convincing poor people that they will share in the fruits of development. Without that conviction, the rural poor are most unwilling and unlikely to make the changes that development may require.

Small farmers and landless laborers are conservative for good reason. They live so close to the bone that innovations can put them at great risk. If a new seed variety fails because of increased susceptibility to pests, or because the government-owned store is short of fertilizer, they and their families face almost certain starvation.

Birth control programs or land reform efforts are both examples of innovations that require profound changes in attitude. Experience has shown that these efforts are successful only when the mass of people have a feeling of participation in the benefits that will come from change. Economic growth, and a just share in the product of that growth, are far more important than absolute levels of income.

Given the fundamental political commitment, much can be done by underdeveloped countries themselves, with their own resources, to feed their people and meet their essential needs. Foreign aid, in the form of oil or food or development capital, can certainly help, but it is up to the Third World countries to make full use of their own resources and those offered by others. They must distribute the food they have equitably, and use it productively. They must plan development so as to create and maintain useful jobs. They must put greater reliance on their own sources of fuel and fertilizer, in order to bridge the gap between the immediate needs of their people and long-term needs of vastly increased food production. And they must demonstrate convincingly that progress and economic growth are for the benefit of all their people.

Notes to Chapter Five

1. William Rich, "Smaller Families through Social and Economic Progress," Monograph No. 7 (Washington, D.C.: Overseas Development Council, 1973).
2. Quoted in Gunnar Myrdal, *Asian Drama* (New York: Pantheon, 1968), p. 1212.

Appendix A

Useful Energy

As far as farm work and irrigation are concerned, we define useful energy as the amount of energy developed at the plow or the shaft of the pump. This definition has in inherent theoretical deficiency in that the theoretical amount of energy to turn the soil, to cut a plant, or to pump water along a horizontal pipe may be much smaller than the energy needed in practice. However, it has a good deal of practical value in that the significant differences in technologies of applying energy to the farm lie in the source of power. A unit of useful energy delivered in a given time to the shaft of a mechanical pump or a tractor is comparable to a unit of useful energy at the shaft of a foot pump or an ox-driven plow.

Of course, the amount of useful energy actually necessary to plow a field or pump water depends on factors such as the type of soil, the depth of plowing, the method of irrigation, the rainfall pattern, the kind of crop, the topography, and the source of the irrigation water. In order to compare energy use in agriculture in different parts of the world, we must take these differences into account. To take differences in farm conditions into account (roughly), we compare only the production of a particular variety of food such as rice or wheat. This does not resolve all the problems such as different seed varieties, but it should eliminate many, but probably not all, major sources of error.

For irrigation we calculate the hypothetical amount of energy that would be necessary if all the irrigation were from an underground water source at a constant depth. The calculation of the actual amount of energy is useful for energy supply considerations and varies greatly from one area to the next. However, this does not appear to explain the major discrepancies that appear in various references. According to Dawson,[1] Chinese planners use a rule of thumb of 0.4 horsepower per hectare for tubewell irrigation, and apparently, the annual power consumption per irrigated hectare is about 250 kwhe. In India, the Rural Electrification Survey[2] reported that the average installed horsepower for tubewell irrigation was about 2 horsepower per hectare and a power consumption of 1800 kwhe/hectare. In Bihar, India, where the water table is often only a few meters deep, the Survey reported about 1.2 horsepower/hectare and an annual power use of 300 kwhe/hectare. In Bihar, at least, it appears that the installed power for tubewell irrigation is seriously underutilized. For many parts of India the Survey may have underestimated the sales of water by owners of pumpsets with the result that the power requirements would tend to be overstated. While we do not have adequate data to comment on the accuracy of the Chinese power estimates for irrigation, it is possible that the lower power requirements in China may partly be attributable to the more even annual distribution of the rainfall, the use of gravity irrigation in hilly areas and perhaps a lower average water table depth. To circumvent these difficulties of data and to compare the effects of irrigation water on crops in energy equivalent terms, we assume a useful energy requirement of 3 million Btu (about 850 kwhe) *per crop* per hectare which is between the Chinese and Indian estimates.[3] Since the actual energy requirements vary greatly from one region to the next, our analysis yields no more than a qualitative idea of the effect of energy used for irrigation. We assume the net efficiency of electricity generation, transmission, distribution and use (in a motor) of 20 percent. We assume the same efficiency (20 percent) for pumps driven by internal combustion engines.

In the U.S., the oil consumption by tractors is about 7 million Btu/ha.[4] This yields useful energy of 1.4 million Btu/ha. at an engine and drive efficiency of 20 percent. For farm animals the calculation is hampered by a lack of field data on annual energy output and the amount of this energy used for various purposes such as plowing, or transportation, or water pumping.

We can arrive at an approximate estimate of the efficiency by noting that (a) the dung output of Third World cattle is between 10 to 15 million Btu;[5] (b) the dung represents between 40 percent and 60 percent of the caloric value of the food intake (Chapter Four); (c) draft cattle and horses develop about one-half horsepower and are used for about 1,000 hours per year. This calculational procedure yields a useful energy output of about 1.2 million Btu (500 horsepower hours) per draft animal per year, or an efficiency of about 5 percent. Morrison[6] cites an efficiency of about 3 percent for U.S. workhorses used for about 1,000 hours per year. Stewart Odend'hal has made some measurements of the work output of draft animals in West Bengal, India.[7] He estimated that draft animals in West Bengal consume about 30 million Btu per year, have a power output of 0.6 to 0.7 horsepower, and work around 1,000 hours per year. These findings are approximately in accord with our assumptions of 0.5 horsepower per animal, and food intake of 25 million Btu per year, and an annual working time of 1,000 hours per year. We will use an efficiency of 5 percent which is higher than Morrison's estimate but approximately in accord with Odend'hal's research. We further assume that, unless otherwise specified, 75 percent of this energy is used for farm operations. If there is one draft animal per hectare (as is common) the annual useful energy in farm operations would be 0.9 million Btu/ha.

The calculation for human labor is similar except that only 40 percent to 50 percent of all human beings are available for work. Unless otherwise specified, we assume that half of the available human labor is used in the fields.

The differences in caloric intake and quality of diet also have an effect on the amount of field work that draft animals or farm laborers can do. Due to a lack of data, we have largely ignored these differences.

For chemical fertilizers, we assume that the amount of useful energy is equal to the amount of energy required to produce the fertilizer. This is not a very satisfactory definition, but we resort to it because of the empirical difficulties associated with using a more rational measure. A rational measure of the usefulness of fertilizer energy (chemical or organic) could be the energy associated with the increase in plant weight due to use of a unit of fertilizer which enables the more efficient capture of solar energy. Thus, if a kilogram of nitrogen causes an increase in wheat yield of five kilograms and an increase in the weight of the crop residue by five kilograms, then the total useful energy output would be about 150,000 Btu. This is to be compared with the 75,000 Btu it takes to manufacture a kilogram of chemical nitrogen fertilizer (nitrogen content).[8] * The manufacture of organic fertilizer in biogasification plants can actually yield efficiently usable energy (methane) as well as fertilizer. The primary empirical difficulty with using this production measure of fertilizer efficiency is that the increase in production has a synergistic effect with irrigation (indeed it is often contingent upon the availability of irrigation water) and it is strongly dependent on the variety of seeds used. Suitably designed field experiments are necessary for the adoption of this measure of fertilizer efficiency. For this book we use the energy required to manufacture a unit of chemical fertilizer as representing useful energy obtained from using fertilizers. In comparing various countries, we attribute the same amount of useful energy output per unit weight of organic fertilizers (unless otherwise specified).

Notes to Appendix A

1. Owen L. Dawson, *Communist China's Agriculture* (New York: Praeger, 1970).
2. Planning Commission, *Report on Evaluation of the Rural Electrification Programme* (New Dehli: Government of India, 1965).
3. David Pimentel et al., "Food Production and the Energy Crisis," *Science* (2 November 1973).

*The energy requirements for the manufacture of potassium and phosphorous fertilizers are much smaller than those for chemical nitrogen since the former are generally obtained from natural deposits.

4. *Ibid.*
5. Harold B. Gotaas, *Composting* (Geneva: World Health Organization, 1956).
6. F. B. Morrisson, *Feeds and Feeding* (Ithaca, N.Y.: Morrisson Publishing Co., 1947).
7. Stewart Odend'hal, "Energetics of Indian Cattle in Their Environment," *Human Ecology* (1972).
8. Pimentel et al., "Food Production."

Appendix B

Biogasification

This appendix gives further information on some technical and economic aspects of biogasification—that is, the production of methane by anaerobic fermentation. We will first discuss the biological aspects of the fermentation. In the second part we will discuss the design of suitable digestor systems.

THE ANAEROBIC FERMENTATION PROCESS

As noted in the main text, anaerobic fermentation is a promising technique for converting organic raw material into a more useful form of energy (in this case, methane). The process is relatively efficient, produces an attractive product, and generates a nutrient-rich effluent which can be recycled to maintain the fertility of the ecosystem producing the raw material. Precise understanding of the process, however, is incomplete, particularly when materials other than sewage are considered. Considerable research must be carried out before an optimal system can be achieved.

General

Anaerobic fermentation is a complex process in which many different micro-organisms act symbiotically. Most organic materials—with the exception of rubbers, waxes, resins, lignin, and some complex hydrocarbons—can be converted to methane (CH_4), carbon dioxide (CO_2), and traces of other gases. The basic conversion steps are illustrated in Figure B–1.

Although this diagram is very simplified, it serves to emphasize the broad division of the process into two phases: an "acid-forming" phase and a "methanogenic" phase. The micro-organisms of the acid-forming phase degrade complex organic compounds such as starches, cellulose, proteins, and lipids, to short-chain fatty acids, alcohols, carbon dioxide, and hydrogen. The micro-

143

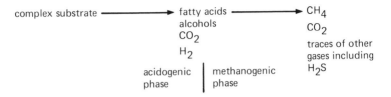

Figure B-1. Basic Conversion Steps in the Anaerobic Methane Fermentation

organisms of the methanogenic phase convert these simple compounds and hydrogen into CH_4 and CO_2.

A variety of simple compounds is produced in the acid-forming phase. Some are:

methanol	acetate
2-propanol	butyrate
butanol	formate
ethanol	lactate
glycerol	propionate
	valerate

The substrates which can be used directly by methanogenic bacteria (defined strictly as micro-organisms producing methane, rather than as micro-organisms in the methanogenic phase) are limited in number. Only methanol, acetate, and carbon dioxide and hydrogen have been indisputably demonstrated to be substrates. Hence, a complex association of micro-organisms is necessary in the methanogenic phase to convert the compounds listed above to substrates for the actual methanogenic bacteria.

A general principle of great importance is that this microbial ecosystem is finely adjusted to a particular steady-state environment. Any abrupt change of any factor in this environment will disrupt the ecosystem, perhaps irreversibly. Hence, changes in nutrient material, the amount of nutrient material, temperature, pH, salinity, and ion concentration should all be minimized, and, if necessary, be introduced gradually.

Many reviews of the microbiology of the methane fermentation exists. Among the most recent are Toerian and Hattingh (1969),[1] and Wolfe (1971),[2] and Pfeffer (1974).[3] Annual reviews of research on the process are to be found in the annual review issues of the *Journal of Water Pollution Control Federation.*

Comparison of the Acid-Forming and Methanogenic Phases

Optimum environments for the two phases appear to be different.[4] The acid-forming phase also appears to be more stable and less fastidious than the methanogenic phase. In sewage treatment the methane-forming step is the rate limiting step in the overall conversion. Growth rates of methanogens are lower (generation time = 4.8 hours) than those of acidogens (generation time = 0.56 hours). It is not clear, however, that the methane-forming step is rate limiting when the material digested is high in cellulose.[5]

Some workers[6,7] suggest physically separating the two phases in order to achieve greater reliability and efficiency.

Conversion Efficiency

Conversion efficiency may be defined as:

$$\frac{\text{Btu methane produced}}{\text{Btu organic matter destroyed}}$$

The consensus among students of biogasification (e.g., Wolfe, 1971) is that 80 percent of the calorific value of degraded material is in the form of methane. It should be emphasized here that conversion efficiency is not the same as net conversion efficiency. Net conversion efficiency is defined as:

$$\frac{\text{Btu methane produced}}{\text{Btu organic matter added}}$$

in which the calorific value of the undigested residuum is accounted for. Under normal conditions, the net conversion efficiency rarely exceeds 65 percent and may vary widely from one material to another.

Kinetics

The kinetics of batch digestion have been described by the equation:

$$P = P_0 (1 - e^{-kt})$$

where:

P   is the cumulative gas production from a unit weight of organic material at a specified time, t

P_O is the ultimate cumulative gas production from a unit weight of organic material after a time long enough for the reaction to come essentially to a close

k is the rate of reaction, expressed as the gas produced in a day as a fraction of the gas remaining to be produced.

Discussions of the kinetics of methane digestion can be found in Imhoff and Fair[8] and Boshoff.[9] Boshoff shows a close correlation between predicted theoretical results and experimental results in Figure B–2. One may note here that both the rate of digestion, k, and the final yield, P_O, are increased by an increase in temperature. Figure B–3 shows the effect that use of different raw materials has on both the rate of digestion and the final yield.

Factors affecting final yield and rate of digestion are, in fact, not entirely understood, but one that has been studied extensively is temperature.

Temperature
There are three basic temperature ranges:

cryophilic   10–25 degrees centigrade
mesophilic   25–40 degrees centigrade
thermophilic   40–60 degrees centigrade

There is fairly general agreement that the rate of digestion, k, increases with temperature. Imhoff and Fair[10] give the following data relating k to temperature in sewage digestion.

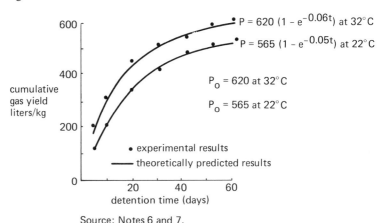

Source: Notes 6 and 7.

Figure B–2. Correlation of Experimental and Theoretically Predicted Cumulative Gas Yield (P), in Batch Digestion of Residue Seeded Elephant Grass

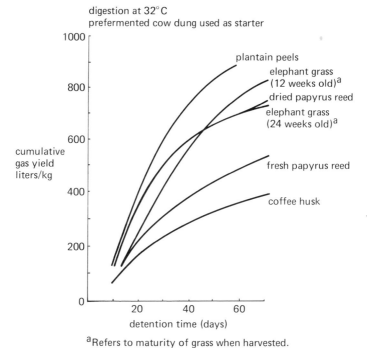

digestion at 32°C
prefermented cow dung used as starter

plantain peels
elephant grass
(12 weeks old)[a]
dried papyrus reed
elephant grass
(24 weeks old)[a]

cumulative
gas yield
liters/kg

fresh papyrus reed

coffee husk

detention time (days)

[a]Refers to maturity of grass when harvested.
Source: Notes 6 and 7.

Figure B-3. Comparative Gas Production from Different Raw
Materials During Batch Digestion

temperature (degrees C)	k
10	0.043
15	0.060
20	0.084
25	0.119
30	0.164

Maly and Fadrus[11] do not use rate but detention time, for gas production from
sewage to come essentially to completion. Their data are:

temperature (degrees C)	detention time (days)
20	80–100
30	33–50
50	20

The conclusion for sewage digestion is, therefore, that the rate of digestion doubles with every increase of 10 degrees centigrade[12] or 15 degrees centigrade.[13] The relationship between k and temperature is not simple, however. As Figure B–4 shows, there is a transition between the mesophilic and the thermophilic range.

Generally speaking, the relationship between rate and temperature holds for other materials, though the evidence available is not complete. A central trade-off in digestor design is between mesophilic and thermophilic cultures (see below). Successful versions of both have been operated for a variety of materials, including the organic component of urban refuse[14,15] grass[16,17] and cattle[18,19] manure.

The effect of temperature on total final gas yield, P_0, is less definite. It would appear that the extent of degradation of different classes of compounds is temperature dependent.[20] Degradation of fats decreases with increasing temperature, whereas that of protein increases with increasing temperature.

	temperature of digestion (degrees C)	
	30	50
degradation of fats (%)	64.9	55.5
degradation of organic nitrogen (%)	57.9	69.1
degradation of organic carbon (%)	55.7	55.8

However, for most materials the variations in yield with temperatures are not

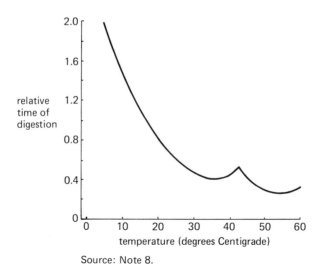

Source: Note 8.

Figure B–4.   Relation of Time of Digestion to Temperature

likely to be significant, at least about 30°C. However, unheated digestors do yield less gas when it gets cold.[21] Heated digestors yield 50 percent more gas and thus achieve a higher net energy conversion efficiency—a matter of importance in many villages where supplies of organic matter inputs may be rather tight relative to fuel needs. To make efficient use of the raw materials, digestors should at least be heated to mesophilic temperatures and maintained at temperatures between 30°–35°C. A sudden stop of even several degrees centigrade can set back the culture for a day or two.

Net Energy Conversion Efficiency

This term was defined earlier in the appendix. In our calculations in the text we have assumed a 60 percent net energy conversion efficiency. As shown in Figure B–3, yields even after a 60-day batch detention time at 32°C can vary substantially from one kind of plant material to another. Boshoff[22] found that the age of plants when harvested, regardless of whether the harvested material was dried, and what size the pieces were to which plant material was chopped, affected the yield. Specifically he found that material dried at room temperature had a higher yield than fresh material (Figure B–3). This finding, if confirmed, should dispel doubts about the validity of storing crop residues for digestion.

The use of a 60 percent net conversion efficiency for crop residues and manure is a reasonable simplifcation, and on the average attainable, given the temperature and detention time which we assumed (32°C, 30-day detention time). Any error involved in choosing between 55 percent and 60 percent efficiency would not be significant given the margin or error in our relatively crude village data.

Singh[23] found that dry leaf powder and fresh manure both yielding about 540 to 580 liters of biogas per kg of dry matter when constant temperatures (over 30°C) were maintained. This approximates a 60 percent net energy conversion efficiency. He reports some surprisingly higher yields for sugarcane thresh and maize straw. In the light of Boshoff's data in Figure B–3, Singh's results for these last two may not be unrealistic. United Aircraft Research Laboratories[24] achieved slightly lower yields for grass clippings and cattle manure with high-rate thermophilic digestion—the yields for both materials were similarly close to one another. Hamilton Standard operated a thermophilic digestor at 8 kg/m^3 digestor volume/day which yielded 620 liters of biogas per kg of volatile solids.[25] Assuming 50 percent CH_4 and 4300 kcal/kg volatile solids, this is equivalent to a net energy conversion efficiency of 65 percent. Varani of Biogas of Colorado, Inc., generally achieves a 55–60 percent efficiency with feedlot manure in the pilot plant operating in Golden, Colorado.[26] In general, inadequate yield data are presently available in reliable published form for the variety of different village materials which may be digested.

It may be useful to point out here that experiments on the digestion of water hyacinth, a very productive aquatic weed which has been cited as a possible additional source of biomass to put in village digestors,[27] have so far been rather disappointing.[28] * While other investigations may reverse these results, they do emphasize the need for specific tests of particular materials, preferably by several different investigators.

Improvement of Net Energy Conversion Efficiency

An improvement in the energy conversion efficiency of the anaerobic methane fermentation would reduce the cost of raw material used per unit volume of methane produced. The effect on the total cost of biogas will depend on the cost of increasing the efficiency versus the savings realized by the resultant decrease in the raw materials required to produce a given amount of gas. As presently developed, the process is moderately efficient, but possibilities for increasing the net conversion efficiency exist. Two will be mentioned here: the development of two-stage digestors and pretreatment of raw material.

The principle of two-stage digestors has been stated earlier. Preliminary results from a two-stage digestor operating at 48°C at the University of Pennsylvania[29] indicate that higher net energy conversion efficiency and higher feed-rates can be achieved with two stage digestors than with single stage digestors. The University of Pennsylvania results are:

	net energy conversion efficiency
single stage digestor at 48°C	48%
single stage digestor at 37°C	55%
two-stage digestor at 48°C	75%

Two-stage digestors are, therefore, a very promising technique, particularly if higher feed-rates can be maintained. Until more data are available, however, it would be premature to either speculate as to why they are more efficient or to assume that the results obtained in the laboratory with simulated solid waste (Purina Dog Chow) can be obtained with plant material. Work on two-stage digestors is presently being carried out at the Institute of Gas Technology in Chicago.

Treatment of indigestible residues may increase digestibility and thus, yield and net conversion efficiency. It has been shown that treatment of

---

*It is for this reason that we assumed that water hyacinths would be used directly as cooking fuel and did not evaluate the economics of using water hyacinths to supply gas for agricultural use.

cow dung[30] and ryegrass straw[31] with sodium hydroxide increases the digestibility of these materials for ruminants. Since the processes in ruminant digestion are similar to those in the methane fermentation, increases in digestibility and yield can be anticipated from treatment of plant material.

The increase in yield is substantial. Smith found that soaking manure for three weeks in a concentrated solution of sodium hydroxide (15 g NaOH/100 g dry matter) resulted in greater than 90 percent digestibility in artificial rumens. That is to say, previously indigestible materials was made almost completely digestible.

Data from Anderson and Ralston[32] are summarized in Table B–1. The degradation of lignin appears to be an important factor in increasing digestibility. Combining this information (bearing in mind that fecal material has a low digestibility, while untreated straw has 30–33 percent digestibility), we may further note that increasing the time that the raw material is soaked in NaOH may increase the digestibility of that material. Since Anderson and

Table B-1. **Effect of Chemical Treatment with NaOH on Digestibility and Chemical Composition of Ryegrass Straw**

(a) Effect of Treatment on Digestibility (Data from Two Experiments)

Treatment Level (g NaOH/100 g Straw)	Mean Digestibility (Percentage)	Percent Improvement over Untreated Straw
No treatment	30.2	–
6	56.2	86.0
8 (approx. 1% solution)	63.2	109.4
10	63.9	111.6
No treatment	33.2	–
15 (2% solution)	67.8	90.5
30 (4% solution)	73.1	105.5
45 (6% solution)	85.5	140.1
60 (8% solution)	90.2	153.4

(b) Effect of Treatment on Levels of Lignin and Crude Protein in Straw

Solution Strength of Treatment (Percentage)	Lignin Percent Decline Below Untreated Straw	Crude Protein Percent Decline Below Untreated Straw
0.5	19.5	7.0
2.0	54.9	30.1
4.0	75.5	43.9
6.0	88.5	69.9
8.0	91.9	72.7

Note: Straw soaked for 24 hours at ambient temperature in NaOH solution; 15 ml solution/g of straw. Straw then dried. Digestibility determined by loading at 1 g/100 ml (10 kg/m^3) in buffered rumen solution at 39° C for 24 hours.

Source: Note 31.

Ralston used treatment times of only 24 hours, this means that a treatment level of 6 g NaOH should produce more than an 86 percent increase in digestibility. If this is the case, then one may suggest that a treatment level lower than that used by Smith (15 g NaOH/100 g fecal dry matter) would result in a very satisfactory increase in digestibility of certain materials.

It is obviously important that the smallest possible amount of NaOH be used for treating the raw material. Therefore, it is logical to confine chemical treatment to the indigestible residue from a methane digestor, if this is possible. The treated residue may then be returned to the digestor. The lignin-rich fibrous mat resulting from digestion of crop residues might be a particularly good candidate for treatment. Contamination and cost are the main constraints, but if sufficiently low treatment levels can be achieved, treatment of residue represents a promising technique for increasing yields. It is possible that with recycling and rinsing, less than 0.5 g of NaOH need be consumed per 100 g dry matter of material. The Institute for Gas Technology is also presently investigating treatment methods.

Approaches other than these may be possible. It has, for example, been suggested that addition of activated charcoal increases the net conversion efficiency for sewage in mixed cultures, and that none of the increases yield is due to digestion of the charcoal. Since we know that ground coal is digestible[33] this claim may be viewed with some skepticism. It is, nevertheless, intriguing.

Some materials (e.g., mercury, antibiotics) are toxic to microorganisms. This problem sometimes causes unreliable operation urban sewage treatment plants because a variety of chemicals and metals are present in the influent. However, the influent to a village biogas plant would be more homogenous and contain fewer toxic materials of the type present in urban sewage treatment plants. Reliable and efficient operation of village biogas plants will require routine maintenance on the part of village level operators and probably frequent inspection and assistance on the part of market town technicians. The training of such operators and technicians must be an important part of any scheme for widespread application of biogas plants. Herbicides, pesticides, and fungicides in high concentrations may also be potentially disruptive, and the effect of increased use of these materials on biogas plant operation should be monitored.

SOME ASPECTS OF THE DESIGN OF
BIOGASIFICATION SYSTEMS

Tank Design

The basic outline of a village biogas-electricity system was presented in Chapter Four. An important variable of the costs in this system are those associated with the conversion of agricultural wastes to gas and the storage of gas. Gas storage capacity is necessary due to the wide fluctuation in hourly and seasonal loads.

The estimated cost of a digestor was shown in Table 4–9 of Chapter Four. The conversion system is assumed to be essentially mesophilic digestion carried out in a vertical-mixing digestor of the type described by Singh.[34] We have selected the mesophilic culture instead of the thermophilic culture because it is the only culture that has been tested in this type of digestor which in turn is the only type of digestor that has been extensively tested under village conditions. The thermophilic process does, however, have some advantages. The rate of digestion is increased since the detention time in the digestor is substantially reduced. As a result a greater quantity of gas is produced per unit of digestor volume and, thus, digestor capital costs per unit output of gas are reduced. Another consequence is that mixing (in digestor designs where this is necessary) requirements are reduced.[35] On the other hand, more heat inputs are required for thermophilic digestion. Pfeffer has presented an interesting discussion of the trade-offs between thermophilic and mesophilic digestors in a recent publication.[36] The choice between mesophilic and thermophilic cultures will be largely influenced by the relative unit costs of digestor volume and heat, both of which are subject to change due to technical improvements. The ease of maintenance is another consideration. Until more data are available for village conditions, it would be premature to speculate on the relative merits of thermophilic and mesophilic cultures.

We have assumed costs per unit volume as found in Prasad, Prasad, and Reddy.*[37] We have assumed a loading rate of 3.2 kg/m³ digestor volume/day or 1050 kg/m³ digestor volume/year (based on Singh[39] assuming a 90 percent load factor to allow for maintenance). For example, in Mangaon this means that a digestor volume of 295 m³ is required to handle about 300 tons per year of manure. It is quite possible that both the volume and the cost per unit volume of the system as costed are too high with the result that our cost estimates are too high.[40] Since biogas-electricity systems compare rather favorably with conventional rural electrification in spite of this overestimate, better digestor design would make such systems even more attractive.

The digestors designed by Singh use concrete walls and a mild steel floating gas holder.[41] These are expensive and probably unnecessary—that is, the digestors are overdesigned. Chlorinated polyethylene, butyl rubber, or other materials could be used to cover and perhaps line the walls of the digestors. An alternative might be to add a bituminous emulsion to earth which is then tamped into the walls. Such emulsions are effectively hydrophobic even at small concentrations and have been used to seal ponds which would otherwise drain away through porous subsoil.

*The costs used by Prasad, Prasad and Reddy appear to be based on Singh's work.[38] Singh's digestors are of the free standing type, and in essence, are simplifications of the digestors used for sewage treatment in many countries.

The loading rate may also be too low, if thermophilic digestion is used. Hamilton Standard produced about 0.25 cubic meters per kilogram of volatile solids in manure[42] with a loading rate of 8 kg per m³ of digestor volume per day. With these rates only 40 percent of the volume assumed for the system in Chapter Four would be required. The construction cost would be reduced approximately in proportion to the reduction in volume. The materials required scale roughly as the two-thirds power of the volume, so that a 60 percent reduction in volume would correspond roughly to a 45 percent reduction in materials. The culture used in this example was thermophilic. The high loading rate used means that this reduction in cost may not all be translated to reduced biogas costs because increasing the loading rate at a given temperature decreases the gas yield, as shown in Figure B–5. The pilot plant of Biogas of Colorado, Inc., operates at approximately the same loading rate as the one we have assumed (3.2 kg/m³/day).

While we do not assume that the residuum is dewatered in this sytem, dewatering may be desirable if the residuum is to be stored for a long time or hauled over long distances (more than a few kilometers). Residuum from the digestion of cattle manure has proven to be remarkably difficult to de-

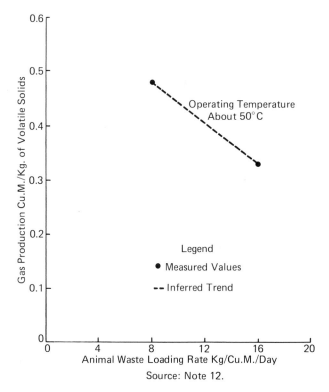

Source: Note 12.

Figure B–5. Gas Production Vs. Loading Rate

water.[43,44] It is possible that lower loading rates, longer detention times, and more complete digestion may improve the dewatering characteristic of cattle manure. F. Varani of Biogas of Colorado found that at a loading rate of 3.2 kg of volatile solids per m^3 per day of digestor volume and a 30-day detention time the residuum dewatered satisfactorily, but at 8 kg per m^3 per day and a 10-day detention time, it was impossible to dewater the residuum.

Another way to reduce costs besides using cheaper construction materials and higher loading rates is to fundamentally redesign the digestors. The most prominent candidate at present is the linear displacement digestor. In the conventional vertical-mixing type common today, material is mixed throughout the volume of the digestor as it is added (in theory). Generally, in order to achieve the necessary circulation, a vertical cylindrical configuration is used.

In a linear displacement digestor, however, the raw material enters at one end of a canal, while the effluent is drawn off from the other end. Material thus flows slowly down the length of the canal, and the movement of the culture approximates a plug flow. Different stages of digestion should predominate at different points along the length of the canal. Gas is drawn off through the roof. Schematic diagrams of a vertical mixing digestor and a linear displacement digestor are shown in Figure B–6. Reduced construction and materials costs are two major advantages of the linear design. (No mixing is assumed, though some may be used). Very simply, it costs less to dig a trench and cover it than to put a hole in the ground, build up load-bearing walls, and cover that. A rough calculation of the cost of a linear displacement digestor equal to the size of that costed in the text (about 300 cubic meters) indicates that the cost per unit volume may be less than 50 percent of the cost of a vertical-mixing type built with steel and cement.

It would be premature to assume that such low-cost digestors are a reality. None have been reported in the standard literature by widely recognized authorities. It has even been suggested that linear displacement or plug flow digestors cannot work, even in theory. However, the theory that predicts that plug flow digestors won't work can be used to show that batch digestors won't work either. But batch digestors definitely do work. Moreover, the small linear digestor built in Golden, Colorado, does produce gas. It is essential that a number of linear displacement digestors of various designs be built as soon as possible and tested. This matter is too important to be left to speculation and the odd pilot plant, or even one demonstration plant. More experimental data are necessary to determine the costs of linear digestors, the gas production rates, and so on. Only such data will enable an accurate comparison between the linear and vertical mising designs.

Carbon Dioxide Removal

CO_2 removal is at present an expensive process for small-scale plants, unless a source of lime is locally available. Therefore, we have not considered CO_2 removal in a village system. CO_2 removal would, of course, improve the

(a) Vertical Mixing Type

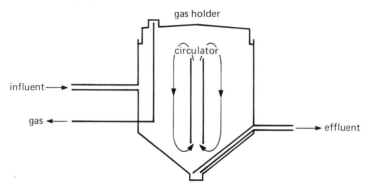

(b) Linear Displacement Type

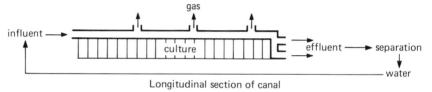

Longitudinal section of canal

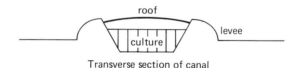

Transverse section of canal

Figure B-6. Schematic Diagrams of the Vertical Mixing and Linear Displacement Digestors (Heating System Not Shown)

economics of gas storage and improve the economics of compressed gas for mobile machinery. When designing CO_2 removal facilities, it should be remembered that only a partial purification would result in significant benefits. It is by no means necessary to purify the gas to "pipeline" standards. Internal combustion engines run well with unscrubbed biogas.[45, 46]

Gas Storage

Gas storage is an essential feature of a biogasification system. Optimum storage capacity can only be accurately determined when digestor unit volume costs, unit storage costs, and the variation in seasonal loads are known.

The basic problem can be illustrated as follows. The economics of digestor operation improve as load factors improve. On the other hand, rural or

digestor operation improve as capacity factors improve. On the other hand, rural or agricultural loads for either gas or electricity are highly variable on both an hourly and seasonal basis, and capacity factors are low. Without storage capacity, the digestor costs would increase by five or six times, and much more careful management would be required to match output with demand. Temporary shut-down of digestors for maintenance or repair could also be very disruptive without some gas storage.

The load patterns for gas will vary from place to place since they depend on the importance and pattern of irrigation use, the number of crops grown, whether cooking gas is part of the system, patterns of machine use, and so on. Storage requirements are related to the number of consecutive days or weeks that output is exceeded by demand, as well as to the level of demand above the annual average.

For example, if there are two periods of equal peak demand separated by three months of zero demand, the storage required would be equal to about 25 percent of total output instead of the 40 percent that would be required if the same demand occurred during one continuous period. It is evident, therefore, that the ratio of storage capacity to total output can be reduced by scattering peak load periods throughout the year. Multiple cropping should have this effect, and its introduction will improve the economics of village biogas plants.

In the analysis in Table 4–9, Chapter Four, a storage capacity of about 40 percent of total gas output was assumed. The unscrubbed gas is stored at 1,500 psi in a lined cylindrical pit (420 m^3), with a reinforced concrete roof costing \$30/m^2.

It may be possible to use abandoned wells for storing biogas, which may reduce the costs of storage.

Heating the Digestor

As discussed in the first section of this appendix, it has been shown that both yield and rate of gas production may be increased by stabilizing the temperature of the digestor at mesophilic or thermophilic temperatures instead of letting it fluctuate with the ambient temperatures. We have also indicated that it might be advantageous to operate at higher themophilic temperatures. An important trade-off here is between the cost of heat and the cost of digestor volume.

The amount of heat required is a function of the operating temperature of the digestor, the temperature of the water entering the digestor, the ambient temperature, and of the quantity of water entering the digestor. Total heat requirements are the sum of (a) the heat loss through the digestor walls and (b) the heat required to bring the influent water up to digestor temperatures. A major factor in determining (a) is the presence or absence of a metal gas holder for the digestor. Eighty percent of the heat loss in conventional sewage digestion is through the metal gas holder.[47] Eliminating or adequately insulating the gas holder will substantially decrease heating requirements.

Recycling of effluent water, with precautions to minimize heat loss during recycling, can result in dramatic saving in heat requirements. Such recycling, however, requires dewatering of the effluent. We are not familiar with dewatering technology and are uncertain regarding its applicability to village systems. We have assumed that during a part of the year effluent water will be introduced directly into irrigation systems, and, during the rest of the year, stored in pits which are inexpensive to excavate. Dewatering might, however, be superior.

If electricity generation and waste heat utilization are combined with biogasification at the outset, it is unlikely that heat supply will be a major problem, though difficulties may be encountered due to intermittent generation on the one hand and the need for reasonably constant heat inputs on the other. Heat requirements are unlikely to exceed 5 or 10 percent of the energy output when digestors are operated at mesophilic temperatures. However, in order to achieve maximum utilization of capital, we have suggested in Chapter Four that electrification may be deferred. In this case, solar heating may be appropriate.

Digestors (particularly those operating at mesophilic temperatures) are in many ways particularly suited to solar heating, particularly in tropical and subtropical latitudes where adequate insulation is available throughout the year. Digestors require only low temperature heat so that simple flat plate collectors will be reasonably efficient. Digestors provide their own thermal storage, so there is little need for any additional heat storage. Solar heating is a feature of the proposed Biogas of Colorado, Inc., plant.

To achieve consistently good gas yields, it may be necessary to install thermostatic controls in village biogas plants. In fuel short areas, every effort should be made to avoid the use of biogas for heating digestors. In other areas, where the supply of organic matter is not a limiting factor in the supply of energy for agriculture, the costs of heating with solar or other systems should be compared with the costs of using biogas since in these cases there is no opportunity cost attached to the use of biogas for digestor heating.

A biogasification system in a village may initially operate at mesophilic temperatures using solar heating. After electrification, some of the waste heat available could be used to operate the digestors at thermophilic temperatures. This may permit digestors of the same volume to convert larger quantities of waste to gas, thus permitting some expansion of fuel-producing capacity without the construction of additional digestors.

Notes to Appendix B

1. D. F. Toerien and W. H. J. Hattingh, "Anaerobic Digestion—I: The Microbiology of Anaerobic Digestion," *Water Research* 3 (1960).
2. R. S. Wolfe, "Microbial Formation of Methane," *Advances in Microbial Physiology* 6 (1971).

3. J. T. Pfeffer, *Reclamation of Energy from Organic Waste,* EPA 670/2-74-016. (Cincinnati, Ohio: National Environmental Research Center Office of Research and Development, Environmental Protection Agency, 1974).

4. F. G. Pohland and S. Ghosh, "Developments in Anaerobic Treatment Processes," in R. P. Canale (ed.), *Biological Waste Treatment* (New York: John Wiley, 1971).

5. Pfeffer, *Reclamation of Energy.*

6. Pohland and Ghosh, "Developments."

7. M. Altmann, "Technology for the Conversion of Solar Energy to Fuel Gas," University of Pennsylvania, University Park, July 1973.

8. K. Imhoff and G. M. Fair, *Sewage Treatment* (New York: John Wiley, 1956).

9. W. H. Boshoff, "Reaction Velocity Constants for Batch Methane Fermentation on Farms," *Journal of Agricultural Science* 68 (1967).

10. Imhoff and Fair, *Sewage Treatment.*

11. J. Maly and H. Fadrus, "Influence of Temperature on Anaerobic Digestion," *Journal of the Water Pollution Control Federation* 43 (1971).

12. Imhoff and Fair, *Sewage Treatment.*

13. Maly and Fadrus, "Influence of Temperature."

14. Imhoff and Fair, *Sewage Treatment.*

15. S. Ghosh and D. L. Klass, "Conversion of Urban Refuse to Substitute Natural Gas by the Biogas^{TM} Process." Paper presented to the Fourth Mineral Waste Utilization Symposium, Chicago, 1974.

16. Ram Bux Singh, *Biogas Plant Generating Methane from Organic Wastes* (Ajitmal, Etawah, Uttar Prodesh, India: Gobar Gas Research Station, 1971).

17. United Aircraft Research Laboratory, *Technology for Conversion of Solar Energy to Fuel* (Washington, D.C.: National Science Foundation, 1974).

18. Singh, *Biogas Plant Generating Methane.*

19. U.S. Department of Agriculture—Hamilton Standard, *Proposal for Thermophilic Fermentation of Feedlot Wastes—Pilot Plant Evaluation* (Washington, D.C.: USDA, 1974).

20. Maly and Fadrus, "Influence of Temperature."

21. Singh, *Biogas Plant Generating Methane.*

22. Boshoff, "Reaction Velocity Constants."

23. Singh, *Biogas Plant Generating Methane.*

24. United Aircraft Research Laboratories, *Technology.*

25. USDA-Hamilton Standard, *Proposal.*

26. F. Varani, Biogas of Colorado, Golden, Colorado, personal communication, 1974.

27. C. R. Prasad, K. Krishna Prasad, and A. K. N. Reddy, "Biogas Plants: Prospects, Problems, and Tasks," *Economic and Political Weekly* (Bombay) (August 1974).

28. United Aircraft Research Laboratories, *Technology.*

29. Altmann, "Technology."

30. L. W. Smith et al., "In Vitro Digestibility of Chemically Treated Animal Feces," *Journal of Animal Science* 31 (1970).
31. Anderson and Ralston, "Chemical Treatment of Ryegrass Straw," *Journal of Animal Science* 37 (1973).
32. *Ibid.*
33. G. E. Johnson, "Production of Methane by Bacterial Action in a Mixture of Coal and Sewage Solids," U.S. Patent 3,640,846, 1972.
34. Singh, *Biogas Plant Generating Methane.*
35. Pfeffer, *Reclamation of Energy.*
36. *Ibid.*
37. Prasad, Prasad, and Reddy, "Biogas Plants."
38. Singh, *Biogas Plant Generating Methane.*
39. *Ibid.*
40. Prasad, Prasad, and Reddy, "Biogas Plants."
41. Singh, *Biogas Plant Generating Methane.*
42. USDA–Hamilton Standard, *Proposal.*
43. S. Ghosh, Institute of Gas Technology, Chicago, personal communication, 1974.
44. W. Jewel, Cornell University, Ithaca, New York, personal communication, 1974.
45. Singh, *Biogas Plant Generating Methane.*
46. Roger Grant et al., Cooperative Extension Service, Pennsylvania State University, University Park, Pennsylvania, personal communication, 1974.
47. L. H. Thompson, Chief Engineer, Sewage Treatment Branch, Public Health Engineering Department, London County Council, London, personal communication, 1973.

Bibliography

Altmann, M. "Technology for the Conversion of Solar Energy to Fuel Gas." University of Pennsylvania, University Park, July 1973.

Anderson and Ralston. "Chemical Treatment of Ryegrass Straw." *Journal of Animal Science* 37.

Best, C. H., and Taylor, N. B. *The Physiological Basis of Medical Practice.* Baltimore, Md.: Williams & Wilkins Company, 1945.

Bienen, Henry. *Tanzania.* Princeton, N.J.: Princeton University Press, 1970.

Boshoff, W. H. "Reaction Velocity Constants for Batch Methane Fermentation on Farms." *Journal of Agricultural Science* 68.

Britannica World Atlas. Encyclopedia Britannica, W. Benton, 1972.

Brown, Lester. *By Bread Alone.* Washington, D.C.: Overseas Development Council, 1974.

Bureau of Mines. *Converting Organic Wastes to Oil.* Washington, D.C.: U. S. Department of the Interior, 1971.

Cambel, A. B., et al. *Energy R&D and National Progress.* Washington, D.C.: U. S. Government Printing Office, 1965.

Crop Reporting Board of the Statistical Reporting Services. *Agricultural Prices.* Washington, D.C.: U. S. Department of Agriculture, September 1974.

Dasmann, R. F., et al. *Ecological Principles of Economic Development.* London: John Wiley & Sons Ltd., 1973.

Dasmann, R. F.; Milton, J. P.; and Freeman, Ph. H. *Ecological Principles for Economic Development.* New York: John Wiley, 1973.

Dawson, Owen. *Communist China's Agriculture.* New York: Praeger, 1970.

Dorner, P. *Land Refore and Economic Development.* New York: Penguin, 1972.

Economic Situation and Prospects for India—Vol. II: The Energy Sector. Washington, D.C.: International Bank for Reconstruction and Development, 1974.

Energy Policy Project. *A Time to Choose: America's Energy Future.* Cambridge, Mass.: Ballinger Publishing Company, 1974.

Etienne, Gilbert. *Studies in Indian Agriculture.* Berkeley: University of California Press, 1968.

"Exposicion en la Reunion Continental sobre la Ciencia y el Hombre." *Energia Electrica en America Latina.* Mexico: Stanford University DF, June 1973.

Fertilizer Statistics 1972-1973. New Dehli: Fertilizer Association of India, December 1973.

Ghosh, S., and Klass, D. L. "Conversion of Urban Refuse to Substitute Natural Gas by the Biogas^{TM} Process." Paper presented at the Fourth Mineral Waste Utilization Symposium, Chicago, 1974.

Gillman, Katherine. "U.S. Energy Use in Historical Perspective." Special staff report of the Energy Policy Project of the Ford Foundation, New York, November 1973.

Gittinger, J. Price. *Economic Analysis of Agricultural Projects.* Baltimore, Md.: Johns Hopkins Press, 1972.

Goodstadt, Leo. *China's Search for Plenty.* New York: John Weatherhill, 1972.

Gotaas, Harold B. *Composting.* Geneva: World Health Organization, 1956.

Gupta, Ranjit. *The Musahri Plan.* Patna, India: Association of Voluntary Agencies for Rural Development, 1972.

Guyol, Nathaniel. *Energy in Perspective of Geography.* Englewood Cliffs, N.J.: Prentice Hall, 1971.

Gyftopoulos, E. P., et al. *Potential Fuel Effectiveness in Industry.* Cambridge, Mass.. Ballinger Publishing Company, 1974.

Harris, Marvin. "The Cultural Ecology of India's Sacred Cattle." *Current Anthropology 7.*

Hass, J. *Financing the Energy Industry.* Cambridge, Mass.: Ballinger Publishing Company, 1974.

Heath, et al. *Land Reform and Social Revolution in Bolivia.* New York: Praeger, 1970.

Hewitt, Cynthia. *The Social and Economic Implications of Large Scale Introduction of New Varieties of Food Grain, Mexico: A Case Study.* Report to the United Nations, in press.

Hill, Polly. *Rural Hausa: A Village and a Setting.* London: Cambridge University Press, 1972.

Imhoff, K., and Fair, G. M. *Sewage Treatment.* New York: John Wiley, 1956.

India 1971–72. New Delhi: Government of India, 1972.

International Research and Technology Corporation. *Problems and Opportunities in the Management of Combustible Solid Wastes.* Washington, D.C.: U.S. Environmental Protection Agency, 1972.

Johnson, G. E. "Production of Methane by Bacterial Action in Mixture of Coal and Sewage Solids." U.S. Patent 3,640, 846, 1972.

Kaiser, E. R., and Friedman, S. B. "The Pyrolysis of Refuse Components." *Combustion.*

Khadi Village Industries Commission. "Gobar Gas—Why and How." Bombay, n.d.

King, F. H. *Farmers of Forty Centuries.* Emmaus, Pa.: Rodale Press, 1911.

Krishna, Raj. "A Model of the Unemployment Trap, with Policy Implications." In *Fiscal Measures for Employment Promotion in Developing Countries.* Geneva: International Labor Office, n.d.

Krishna, Raj. "Measurement of the Direct and Indirect Employment Effects of Agricultural Growth with Technical Change." In *Externalities in the Transformation of Agriculture.* Ames: Iowa State University, in press.

Krishna, Raj. "Unemployment in India." *Indian Journal of Agricultural Economics* 28.

Kuo, Leslie. *The Technical Transformation of Communist China's Agriculture.* New York: Praeger, 1972.

Liebeskind, Judith E. "Pyrolysis for Solid Waste Management." *Chemtech,* September 1973, pp. 537–542.

Long Term Economic Growth, 1860–1970. Washington, D.C.: U.S. Bureau of Economic Analysis, U.S. Department of Commerce, 1973.

Makhijani, A. B., and Lichtenberg, A. J. "An Assessment of Energy and Materials Utilization in the U.S.A." Electronics Research Laboratory Memorandum ERL-310 (rev.), University of California, Berkeley, September 1971.

Maly, J., and Fadrus, H. "Influence of Temperature on Anaerobic Digestion." *Journal of the Water Pollution Control Federation* 43.

Mao Tse-Tung. *Selected Works of Mao Tse-Tung.* Peking: Foreign Languages Press.

Mellor, John. "Report on Technological Advance in Indian Agriculture as It Relates to the Distribution of Income." International Bank for Reconstruction and Development, December 1969.

Mellor, John, et al. *Developing Rural India.* Bombay: Lalvani Publishers, 1972.

Morrisson, F. B. *Feeds and Feeding.* Ithaca, N.Y.: Morrisson Publishing Co., 1947.

Mudahar, Mohinder S. "Dynamic Analysis of Agricultural Revolution in Punjab, India." Cornell University, Ithaca, New York, July 1974.

Muller, Ronald. "Poverty is the Product." *Foreign Policy* 13: 71-103.

Myrdal, Gunnar. *Asian Drama.* New York: Pantheon, 1968.

National Council for Applied Economic Research. *Market Towns and Spatial Development in India.* New Dehli: NCAER, 1965

Netschert, Bruce, et al. *Energy in the American Economy 1850–1975.* Baltimore, Md.: Johns Hopkins Press, 1960.

"1973: The Year of Major Changes in Worldwide Oil." *Gas and Oil Journal* 71.

Nyerere, Mwalimu. *The Arusha Declaration.* Washington, D.C.: Embassy of Tanzania, n.d.

Odend'hal, Stewart. "Energetics of Indian Cattle in Their Environment." *Human Ecology* 1.

Oil Shale Utilization: Progress and Prospects. New York: United Nations, 1967.

Openshaw, Keith. "Projections of Wood Use in Tanzania." Unpublished report to the Public Works Department, Tanzania, Midlothian, Great Britain, 1973.

Openshaw, Keith. "Projections of Wood Use in Thailand." Unpublished report to the Public Works Department, Thailand, Midlothian, Great Britain, 1973.

Openshaw, Keith. "The Gambia: A Wood Consumption Survey and Timber Trend Study 1973–2000." Unpublished report to the ODA/LRD Gambia Land Resources Development Project, Midlothian, Great Britain, 1973.

Owen, D. F. *Man in Tropical Africa.* New York: Oxford University Press, 1973.

Owens, Edgar, and Shaw, Robert. *Development Reconsidered.* Lexington, Mass.: D. C. Heath and Company, 1972.

Pimenthel, David, et al. "Food Production and the Energy Crisis." *Science*, 2 November 1973.

Pfeffer, J. T. *Reclamation of Energy from Organic Waste.* EPA 670/2-74-016. Cincinnati, Ohio: National Environmental Research Center Office of Research and Development, Environmental Protection Agency, 1974.

Pohland, F. G., and Ghosh, S. "Developments in Anaerobic Treatment Processes." In *Biological Waste Treatment* edited by R. P. Canale. New York: John Wiley, 1971.

Planning Commission. *Approach to the Fifth Plan.* New Delhi: Government of India, 1973.

Planning Commission. *Report on Evaluation of Rural Electrification in India.* New Delhi: Government of India, 1965.

Poole, Alan. "The Potential for Energy Recovery from Organic Wastes." In *The Energy Conservation Papers* edited by Robert H. Williams. Cambridge, Mass.: Ballinger Publishing Company, 1975.

Power Study of South Central Brazil. Nassau, Bahamas: Canambra Engineering Consultants Limited, 1966.

Prasad, C. R.; Prasad, K. Krishna; and Reddy, A. K. N. "Biogas Plants; Prospects, Problems, and Tasks." *Economic and Political Weekly* (Bombay), August 1974.

Production Yearbook 1972. Vol. 26. Rome: Food and Agriculture Organization of the United Nations, 1973.

Prothero, R. M., ed. *A Geography of Africa.* London: Routledge & Keagan Paul, 1973.

Rao, K. L. "Irrigation." New Delhi: Government of India, 1972.

Report of the Energy Survey of India Committee. New Delhi: Government of India, 1965.

Rich, William. "Smaller Families Through Social and Economic Progress." Monograph No. 7. Washington, D.C.: Overseas Development Council, 1973.

Richardson, S. D. *Forestry in Communist China.* Baltimore, Md.: Johns Hopkins Press, 1966.

Robert Morey Associates (Dana Point, California). *Energy Information* 9:2.

Roger Revelle et al. "Water and Land," Chapter 7 in *The World Food Problem,* Vol. II, U.S. Government Printing Office, Washington, D.C., 1967.

Saolapurka, V. K., and Balkundi, S.V. *Rice.* New Delhi: Fertilizer Association of India. 1969.

Sen, L. K., et al. *Planning Rural Growth Centers for Integrated Area Development.* Hyderabad, India; National Institute for Community Development, 1971.

Serra, Jose. *El Milagro Brasilero: Realidad o Mito.* Santiago de Chile: Quimantu, 1971.

Shaw, Robert. "Jobs and Agricultural Development." Monograph No. 3. Washington, D.C.: Overseas Development Council, 1970.

Sidel, Victor, and Sidel, Ruth. "The Delivery of Medical Care in China." *Scientific American* 230: 1927.

Singh, Ram Bux. *Biogas Plants.* Ajitmal, Etawah, Uttar Pradesh: Gabar Gas Institute, 1971.

Smith, L. W., et al. "In Vitro Digestibility of Chemically Treated Animal Feces." *Journal of Animal Science* 31.

"Soil and Water." In *The President's Report of Agriculture.* Washington, D.C.: U.S. Government Printing Office, n.d.

Southworth, Herman, ed. *Farm Mechanization in East Asia.* New York: Agricultural Development Council, 1972.

Stamp, Dudley. *Asia.* New York: E. P. Dutton & Co., 1958.

Stanford Research Institute. *Effective Utilization of Solar Energy to Produce Clean Fuel.* Washington, D.C.: National Science Foundation, 1974.

Stoner, Carol H., ed. *Make Your Own Power.* Emmaus, Pa.: Rodale Press, 1974.

Swazambu, S. "Power Development." New Delhi: Government of India, 1972.

Tabor, H. "Solar Energy Utilization." Paper presented at the Interregional Seminar on Rural Electrification (of the United Nations), New Delhi, August 1971.

Tanganyika Central Statistical Bureau. *Village Economic Surveys, 1961–1962.*

Toerien, D. F., and Hattingh, W. H. J. "Anaerobic Digestion–I: The Microbiology of Anaerobic Digestion." *Water Research* 3.

United Aircraft Research Laboratory. *Technology of Conversion of Solar Energy to Fuel.* Washington, D.C.: National Science Foundation, 1974.

U.S. Cattle and Livestock Statistics. Washington, D.C.: U.S. Department of Agriculture, n.d.

U.S. Department of Agriculture–Hamilton Standard. *Proposal for Thermophilic Fermentation of Feedlot Wastes–Pilot Plant Evaluation.* Washington, D.C.: USDA, 1974.

van der Schalie, H. "World Health Organization Project, Egypt 10–A Case History of a Schistosomiasis Control Project." In *The Careless Technology* edited by M. Taghi Farvar and J. P. Milton. Garden City, N.Y.: The Natural History Press, 1972.

Village Technology Handbook. Mt. Rainier, Md.: Volunteers in Technical Assistance, Inc., 1973.

Wang, You-Tsao. "Farm Mechanication in Taiwan: Its Problems and Research Needs." In *Farm Mechanication in East Asia* edited by H. Southworth. New York: Agricultural Development Council, 1972.

Wilkie, R. *San Miguel: A Mexican Collective Ejido.* Stanford, Calif.: Stanford University Press, 1971.

Williams, Robert H., ed. *The Energy Conservation Papers.* Cambridge, Mass.: Ballinger Publishing Company, 1975.

Wolfe, R. S. "Microbial Formation of Methane." *Advances in Microbial Physiology* 6.

World Bank. "Additional Capital Requirements of Developing Countries." Washington, D.C., March 1974.

World Energy Supplies 1960–1970. Statistical Papers, Series J. No. 15. New York: United Nations, 1971.

Index

'ING ALFRED'S COLLEGE
LIBRARY